Discovery Teaching Like Jesus

Engaging Adult Learners

Discovery Teaching Like Jesus
Engaging Adult Learners

Kathy Hoppe

&

Jeff Hoppe

Discovery Teaching Like Jesus Copyright © 2019 Kathy & Jeff Hoppe
All rights reserved.
ISBN-13:9781699000182

DEDICATION

This is dedicated to our teachers
who taught us how to be adult learners,
and to our students who showed us
how to be adult teachers.

CONTENTS

Preface

Acknowledgements

PART I	**WHAT'S GOING ON?**	1
CHAPTER 1	THOUGHTFUL OBSERVATIONS	4
CHAPTER 2	ADULT LEARNING	11

PART II	**A DIFFERENT WAY**	27
CHAPTER 3	DISCOVERY IN TEACHING	29

PART III	**TRY THIS INSTEAD**	42
CHAPTER 4	CREATE TEACHABLE MOMENTS	42
CHAPTER 5	EMPLOY POWERFUL NARRATIVES	52
CHAPTER 6	SPARK CURIOSITY	58
CHAPTER 7	MAKE THEM THINK	72
CHAPTER 8	HOW DOES THIS WORK?	79

PART IV	**BEING EXCELLENT**	93
CHAPTER 9	WHOSE NEED DOES IT MEET?	97

| CHAPTER 10 | INNER & OUTER ATTENDING | 103 |
| CHAPTER 11 | TRAINING & SUPPORTING REFLECTIVE TEACHERS | 110 |

Bibliography   119

About the Authors   127

Preface

Once upon a time a girl and a boy met in the Lone Star state while attending a staff retreat. They were caught off-guard because little did they know this would mark the beginning of their journey together. She was fascinated with his way of communicating clearly and concisely about theological systems and his understanding of biblical truths. He was surprised by her mind. The other girls he met did not ponder things so deeply. While they spent the year working on different college campuses and commuting to other meetings together, they began to talk about life, relationships, religion, and many other topics. Sometimes the drives were not long enough. And when they found one another at the seminary campus, there was nothing that could separate them from continuing their conversations. And, that dialogue continues to this day.

Some people do not like the way we question everything. We believe we embrace a healthy skepticism. In this book, we use our critical reflection skills and practical experiences to guide readers through learning how to engage adults in religious and spiritual education. Some of you may not like our methods. Others are going to love it. Do what you will with this book. You may think that we are wrong, but if we spur you to reflect more deeply about how to teach adults, then we have accomplished our purpose.

In this model, *Discovery Teaching Like Jesus,* we propose that Jesus demonstrates how we need to interact with adults so that they can have a transformational experience. In Part I, we introduce you to our observations. It is not our intent to be critical but rather to critique current teaching methods in our churches. We do so from our own training and experiences. We do not claim to be experts the field of adult education, but we do have exposure and experience in leading adult groups.

In Part II, we introduce you to a different way of teaching, that of discovery learning. We use examples from the ministry of Jesus to demonstrate the principles we promote. In Part III, we dissect these elements for you so readers can learn how to create teachable moments, employ powerful narratives, spark curiosity, and make adults think. Then we provide you with our ideas and resources to implement the model. Finally, in Part IV, we talk about excellence, motivation, self-reflection and self-supervision, as well as training and support for reflective leaders.

Throughout this book, the scriptures are quoted from the New International Version. While some of our experiences are individual, we're combined those into a corporate voice for easier reading.

Thanks for reading. We wish you success in your ministry to adults. Blessings, *Kathy & Jeff Hoppe*

Acknowledgments

We have so many people to thank in working on this project. First, to our former professor, Dr. William Hendricks, who valued our input as students and later as professional ministers and counselors, we are deeply grateful for your influence. We are also thankful for our other instructors and professors who allowed us to question, ramble, pontificate, and who simply would not allow us to settle for naïve answers. For our ACPE supervisors, you deserve more credit than you receive. You taught us the value of self-reflection and we continue to learn from those experiences.

We owe a special thanks to Dr. HeeKap Lee, associate professor of teacher education at Azusa Pacific University and author of *Faith Based Education that Constructs,* for reading our manuscript and offering valuable suggestions. Several other people read sections of this book and provided guidance, advice, and feedback. Thank you to Rev. Jeremy Skaggs, Senior Minister of The Welcome Table Christian Church in Arlington, TX; Deneise Dillon, Executive Director Emeritus of Dillon International in Tulsa, OK; and Penny Fowler Sheehan, retired educator, Collinsville, OK.

We are so happy to participate in a community group presently that welcomes and practices what we promote here. Thank you, *Oikos,* for receiving and accepting us. We know that you are swimming upstream in a system that does not yet understand what you're trying to accomplish or how essential your group is to healthy adult spiritual formation.

We must thank our sons for their patience with us as they grew up hearing us debate one Sunday after another about the lessons we heard. At times we were unfairly critical and other times were simply searching for our own beliefs. We hope that our exploration enhanced your own spiritual growth and continually pray that you will find the Holy One present in your lives and families.

PART I
WHAT'S GOING ON?

"To what can I compare this generation" (Mt. 11:16)?

Sitting in the back of the theology class, we looked around to see some students furiously writing notes in the margin of their notebooks, while others were huddled together in discussion, and yet several peers had their hands raised. Our eyes were full of wonder at this person we called "Doctor," the professor of the class. The experience of being in his classroom was a thrill and left us to marvel, even years later, what made this person's teaching so exciting that students crowded his courses and wanted to continue the discussion with him long after the dismissal. We remember this professor with great fondness who continued to remain in our lives over the next 20 years, and from whom we are still learning.

In seminary, we found the books dull and tedious. Overwhelmed with the amount of reading, it was often hard to digest all the information. But we wanted to be ministers and that required that we obtain graduate theology degrees. We both had good backgrounds as committed Christians, each growing up in churches where we attended weekly Sunday school, learning the Bible inside and out, becoming committed followers, and discipling others. Both of us had worked in churches and on college campuses teaching Bible studies and focusing on evangelistic activities. We had a solid foundation for entering the seminary experience.

We thought we were prepared for the educational process. But the first week's reading for Old Testament included reading the books of the Pentateuch and the first 75 pages of a book on biblical criticism that made reading the obituaries more fun. Then we would attend a class in church administration where even the brightest students struggled to keep their eyes open. We thrashed our way through Greek and Hebrew, endured the preaching class, and found our way to the voluminous reference materials in the library. So, to find a teacher that could capture our attention and hearts was quite amazing.

Looking back on it, we recall this professor's unique mannerisms and how he phrased things, mispronouncing words by placing enunciation on non-dominant syllables and using pithy statements. His application of artistry to theology and his travels around the world became part of the stories he told. We laughed, as he seemed to chase rabbits during lectures only to discover the pertinence of the information on the next exam. Not one word was wasted. He chose his words carefully but more than anything, he treated us like we could think. And he showed a genuine interest in our lives, what we were doing, inviting us to his home to discuss a current movie and theology, or asking us to help with a dinner for distinguished guests, or writing a poem for a student's ordination service. Then he sent us Christmas cards with letters until his death. That left an indelible impression on us. He taught us how to teach by demonstrating a model of discovery.

This type of teaching provides a solid foundation for us as we continue our journey as educators, chaplains, ministers, and counselors. Our desire is to introduce and encourage a style of teaching that is dynamic, that allows ample room for participant voices, and casts a vision for other teachers as they lead adults in spiritual formation. To demonstrate this system, we must first deconstruct a method that is not working well.

CHAPTER 1
THOUGHTFUL OBSERVATIONS

"What did you go out into the wilderness to see" (Mt. 11:7)?

Our journey of teaching and motivating learners has taken us to various parts of the United States. Moving from the cosmopolitan area of San Francisco to the harsh winters of North Dakota, and then on to hot summers in Texas and Oklahoma, we worked in ministry and volunteered where we were able. From there, we traveled and trained others in the mountains of Pennsylvania and the Land of Enchantment (New Mexico). We taught in Sunday school, in churches, at retreats, on college campuses, in small and large groups, and online platforms. This journey of education and studying exposed us to variant forms of instruction, both good and not so good.

Many times, we were the participants sitting in classes, most often in church settings. Some were informative, some boring, and some were disappointing. We marveled at how many leaders had no idea how to teach adults. They lectured or preached at us. We entered classes labeled as discussion only to find very little was encouraged, and sometimes our questions were held in disdain as interruptive processes to the lesson. At times we kept silent and other times said too much, forsaking the acceptance of teacher and peers in our efforts to be honest and truthful.

One time, we asked a question about the scripture passage. It was speculative but provocative. The scripture passage was troublesome, seemingly indicative of discriminatory and abusive practices. We would not accept the platitudes offered but continued to query in different ways until the teacher grew silent, and someone raised the Bible and accused us of not believing in "the word of God." But that's not what we were trying to communicate (we wholeheartedly believe in the truths of scripture). We were trying to engage the communal thoughts of the group to examine the meaning and purpose of this passage, and how that translates into Christian practice.

There were other times when we would leave class early, frustrated at the lack of skill, and what seemed to be either indoctrination of the audience or the narrow focus of what the instructor professed to be the truth. We remember times when we both looked at one another as if to say, "We've had enough," and leave the session. And yet the feeling that we were judgmental was troublesome. We wanted to pull these teachers aside and let them know of the endless spiritual formative possibilities for the people and themselves personally. Just a few tips might help them, but instead, we often slid out early, never revisiting the class.

In our 38 years together, we have participated in thousands of hours of classes and taught as many. We know that we have different gifts in teaching. We have expertise in asking insightful questions, facilitating discussion, and using experiential practices that solidify the lessons. Our abilities in organizing and presenting complex information and the use of creativity help bring classes alive in dialogue. The combination of our teaching skills helps to change lives. Lest anyone should think that we are vain, it does not come from hubris. We desire that people experience transformative lessons.

There are times when we have been in settings that honor adult learning, bringing an understanding that changed us. These are experiences that remain with us through the years and continue to teach us as we reflect on them. Recently Kathy accidentally attended a workshop where new ideas surfaced. Having signed up for something different, her friends swept her away amid her groaning to enjoy a session on the use of poetry as a therapeutic medium. While the leaders spoke of their use of lyrics and metaphors with struggling people, they encouraged participants to write a haiku. The conference speakers then informed the crowd that participants could share at the end of the session. As Kathy started her writing, an impression surfaced that ripened into a lesson that she could carry outside of the seminar. Here's the haiku that Kathy wrote and shared with the group:

At first glance of sun
The light reveals the truth
That fades by noonday.

Simplistic, isn't it? One would think this poem is merely about sunrise, but it's so much more than that. It speaks to the vulnerability of humans who begin to share their inner world, briefly exposing themselves, but then receding away from disclosure in the act of protection. It communicates both the courage and difficulty in exposing one's self to others. Writing this reveals insecurity and fear of judgment and points in the direction of either shrinking from openness or finding a resolution. How can she accomplish this? Now her journey includes a practice of self-reflection on how to trust God's timing and discerning appropriate moments to share her thoughts.

Had it not been for Kathy's unintentional visit to this class, she would never have opened this door. Had it not been for the safety created by the leaders that all participants could do this, that no one would judge one another, and that praise would be shared to everyone for their efforts, this discovery would remain hidden. Whether the teachers were aware or not, they changed Kathy's thoughts about how she could be both honest and self-protective. And they did the same for all who chose to share their poetry. All left with enthusiasm and wonder at how something simple could alter their perceptions and teach them to be better in their work in counseling people.

Other times we have expressed how the group process has opened new pathways for our students and us. When we first experienced truthful groups, such as process or interpersonal relationship meetings, we were shocked at how they confronted us. Even during anxiety and discouragement, the members' ability to call out our insecurities and need for approval, or control, or lack of self-awareness, left us feeling worn out but incalculably changed by the discourse. In turn, this changed our focus in ministry and moved us to a place of helping pastors and therapists to examine their calling, their purpose, and their ministry.

As we look back on our ministries, we know that the measure of success is not in the number of churches we led, or the number of people at those, or any degree, award, or certificate that we garnered. What we achieved in our near 40 years of service is evident in those who were our students. Our students are followers of Christ, present in every corner of the world, receiving awards, and touching many lives. When we hear of former students' successes, we revel in that, knowing we had some small part in their spiritual journey.

We have been present in learning situations that discourage and de-motivate people. We have also been humbled to be in the presence of those who know how to impassion others. The lessons we have learned remain with us. That is what it means to be a lifelong pupil, and that is what we desire for the church to be – a place of enduring learning. This book is designed to be an inspirational tool for teachers to rethink how they guide students to grow in Christ.

Imagine with us. What might it be like to have classes brimming with excitement as people gather together, sharing what God is doing in their lives, and how God is using them to relay the Gospel message in a world longing for authentic connection? Picture the lesson not ending when the clock chimes, but rather the conversation continuing down the halls and out the doors, making its way into the neighbor's house at dinner or weaving its way into an office workspace. Envision a participant reflecting on the lesson and making a life-changing decision that impacts faith and family, and that touches one's heart, mind, and body. This excitement occurs in the discovery teaching of Jesus.

Reflection

If we are true to our theory and beliefs, we cannot move forward until we ask you, adult learners, to stop and reflect on the reading thus far. At the end of each chapter, we pose some questions for you.

1. Think about your experience of learning in your religious or church community. In what ways has it been helpful? What barriers have you faced?

_____
_____
_____

2. What do you enjoy most about learning? What types of experiences challenge you to grow?

_____
_____
_____

3. What teacher has been the most inspiring to you spiritually? What was it about them or their teaching that captured your attention?

_____
_____
_____

CHAPTER 2
ADULT LEARNING

"Do you see all these things" (Mt. 24:2)?

What are we doing? It's a curious question, or so it seems. What *are* we trying to accomplish in our churches these days? What is the purpose of the lesson in Sunday school, Bible study, or group studies? Is the intention to teach dogma, or is it to ensure that people follow the overt and covert rules of a congregation or parish? We are uncertain of the church's goals anymore. Is it to increase the number of people attending? Or is it to evangelize, winning people to Jesus (which we are all in favor of)? Being educators, we desire that people draw near to God and grow in Christ. We propose that the mastery of Christian knowledge should take us on a journey of discovery and lead us to change the lives around us, including our own.

As we reflect on what we see and hear, we realize that some educational mistakes are occurring in our churches. We don't believe these are the result of poor leadership or poor planning, but rather a lack of understanding and knowledge of adult learning. We trust most churches have the best intentions. The key problem lies in a misunderstanding about our assumptions of how adults learn. Once we understand adults correctly and equip teachers with appropriate competencies, then our churches will be providing quality spiritual formation. We discuss the assumptions of adult learning in this chapter and in Part IV will discuss instructor skills, including disposition.

In current practices within the church setting, the theory and methodology of teaching pull us apart and away from becoming competent believers. Some of the common mistakes we notice in our observations of teaching fall into several categories: inadequate theories about the process of adult learning, incorrect methodology, and little or incomplete training. How can we begin to change the way we practice adult education in religious settings? We must move from simply conveying information to learners, providing direct instruction, away from memorization and recitation, and instead move adults towards constructing knowledge, providing inquiry-based instruction, engaging them in revision of core beliefs, and then applying those to their life to achieve transformation (Lee, personal communication, 2019). It is, therefore, important to discuss mistakes occurring in ministry settings related to theories of adult learning, methodology, and training of leaders.

Mistakes of Theory

To understand where we need to go, we must acknowledge where we are off track in religious adult education. We do not expect that leaders of adult classes necessarily have degrees in education. Still, it is crucial for them to understand different adult learning theories and the implications of those. Commonly we notice that many churches use theories of learning that are not well suited for adult spiritual formation. We believe this is due to a lack of understanding or knowledge about such theories.

Most teaching falls within three perspectives: behaviorism, cognitivism, and constructivism (Chowdhury, 2006). The behavioral theory is commonly used in education settings and aims at modifying behavior, or conditioning behavior, and does so through reinforcement (either positive or negative). An example in adult education would be the acknowledgment of a learner's stated words (positive reinforcement), which then communicates to all other students the appropriate form of learning in that setting. However, negative reinforcement is also used, and most commonly is done when the leader either responds with silence or redirection. Behaviorism works well in managing systems and produces satisfaction in adult learners who, upon pleasing the teacher, receive affirmation. However, the weakness is that behaviorism is unable to address the complexities of humans and ignores the cognitive processes of adults (Espinor, 2010).

Behaviorism is present in ministry settings as information is imparted in the same way each week with little innovation and practically no room for discourse. Often the leader seeks agreement, focusing on conformity in religious belief (positive reinforcement) and disdaining any ideology that would disagree (negative reinforcement). When people offer a different opinion, the typical response is either redirection to the main goal, or a rebuff, or silence (negative reinforcement). The goal is to manage the process and keep everyone comfortable. This response acts to consolidate a group and quickly dismisses or "weeds out" those who will not fit the group expectations. That leaves those who desire discussion and critical reflection to move on to another class. When the adults find that each assembly has the same norming pattern, they resign themselves and forego any structured adult interaction that might enhance their spiritual growth.

Cognitive theories focus on the acquisition of knowledge, and the goal is to transfer information from an "expert" to a "novice" (Chowdhury, 2006). This theory recognizes that humans have the capacity for attention, perception, and connection of data, leading to problem-solving. The strength of this theory is that both the expert and novice can collaborate, while the weakness is the neglect of behavioral alterations that are necessary for lasting change (Espinor, 2010).

In the church setting, the cognitive theory is present in the assumption that adults merely want to listen and absorb biblical stories. It leads to a teaching model that is lecture-oriented, and with that indoctrination may follow. The leader has someone read the scripture and tells the group the meaning of the bible passage. There may be a question or two, but those are intended to move to the understanding that the leader intends, and not necessarily towards self-development. More often than not, the teacher provides direct answers to the questions, or the person in charge disregards the query or returns to the proclamation of what he or she believes the audience needs to know. It's a simple plan that keeps everyone on the path of the leader's objectives for that day. The problem with this approach, from our perspective, is that it does not encourage the learner to explore other options and encourages a rigid thinking style that causes dissonance when the Christian confronts life's difficulties. In these settings, teachers who attempt to encourage in-depth exploration may be censored by religious leaders who fear those discussions will lead someone astray from the acceptable church dogma.

Constructivism encourages a more open-ended experience. It primarily focuses on the learner creating meaning based on experience, beliefs, and knowledge gained through listening, analyzing, formulating hypotheses, attempting to practice, and implementing new understanding (Chowdhury, 2006). The strength is that it views humans holistically, having both the capacity for thinking and changing behaviors. The weakness of constructivism is that leaders possibly lose control of the class, and viewpoints arise that do not align with an organization's values, ethics, or doctrine (Espinosa, 2010). Many churches fear this path. What if people come to church and leave thinking something antithetical to the church? Or what if we lead people astray when we allow these types of discussion? Those are valid concerns of any ministry leader.

The question remains, are we treating our adults like they can receive information, question it, and then apply it? If we think that they cannot do this, then we end up spoon-feeding them. Heiland and Hjalmarson say,

> We don't merely believe our way into spirituality. We must practice our way. Knowledge without action stunts spiritual growth. We can listen to sermons and attend good Bible studies, but until we put Christian truth into practice, little transformation will occur" (2011, p. 93).

The current practice of religious adult education builds a dependency upon the instructor and possibly infers that adults cannot function without such a leader. But they can, can't they? Don't we want our Christian brothers and sisters to go into the world and make the right decisions? We believe the church desires for Christians to bring Christ into the world to redeem it. But how can they do this if they're only informed *what* to think instead of *how* to think? How can they possibly be difference-makers in the world if they need constant direction from another source?

Mistakes of Methodology

While learning theories guide the direction of our journey, teaching models provide the vehicle. Whenever leaders are poorly informed about theoretical perspectives, they tend to adopt approaches without discerning if those fit the audience. This is like choosing a tugboat to cross an ocean. It works initially, but eventually will lose power in the implementation. That means we will not arrive where we aim.

The first mistake of practice is the use of pedagogy with adults rather than andragogy. So, what's the difference? Pedagogy assumes the learner is dependent upon the instructor, is unaware of what he or she needs to know, that students are motivated to learn by a force outside them, and that the previous experience of the student is irrelevant (Ozuah, 2005). Pedagogy is often the practice of teaching children and adolescents who are in earlier stages of maturity. Depending on one's theory of human development, one can identify differences in learning needs and styles. Children need explicit instruction, modeling, repetition, and practice. When they become adolescents, they need to obtain skills that require critical thinking.

Most educators are familiar with Bloom's Taxonomy (Bloom, 1956). In the late 50s, Benjamin Bloom and his colleagues developed this framework for categorizing education goals. It was revised in 2001 and currently has six categories of skills and abilities that describe the cognitive process necessary for learning (Armstrong, 2016). These are fashioned into a pyramid. The bottom level of the pyramid pertains to knowledge acquisition through remembering as characterized by recognition and recall. The next level aims at comprehension as exhibited when a student interprets, classifies, summarizes, infers, compares, or explains. The third level aims at application, such as when a student takes the information and implements it.

At the fourth level, the learner begins to analyze information when they organize or prioritize, or differentiate. The fifth level of knowledge involves evaluation or synthesis when a student checks and critiques the data and places elements together to form a whole picture. Finally, the highest level of knowledge occurs when students create. They generate, plan, and produce new concepts (Armstrong, 2016). The goal of education begins at the lowest level and uses a variety of methods and as a person matures, teachers challenge students to continue growing in their knowledge and understanding by presenting tasks that shifts learning to the next level of understanding.

The lowest levels of learning involve memory or recall of basic data (Bloom, 1956). That's why children need a lot of replication and rehearsal. They also need clear explanations so they can understand the principles. As such, they may spend time reading and memorizing information and then using activities to test their recall. As children grow, they can move to the application of principles, learning to use facts in new ways. Moving into adolescence, we teach teens to analyze material by having them compare ideas and learning to question instead of readily accepting proofs placed before them. By the time teens reach adulthood, they need to know how to evaluate, synthesize material, and create new solutions (Armstrong, 2016). We are doing well as teachers of children and adolescents if we lead them in this direction.

Andragogy makes different assumptions. Adults need to know why something is important to learn. Without this, few adults have the desire or motivation to undertake the formation process. Other pertinent assumptions that differ from children and teens include the adult's self-concept, i.e., bearing responsibility for life decisions, and the role of experience. Adults bring a wider variety and a different quality of interest from life's encounters and seek to incorporate information within that frame of reference. Adults, therefore, come ready to learn when doing so helps them cope more effectively in real life situations. This leads to the next two assumptions about adult learning. Adults are life-centered and desire that learning enhance their well-being. They are motivated by internal pressures such as self-esteem, quality of life, and a desire for increased life satisfaction (Lee, personal communication, 2019).

Malcolm Knowles labels adults as self-directed learners (Knowles, Holton, & Swanson, 1998). In his work, Knowles makes some assumptions about adults: as maturation occurs, the adult self-concept moves from dependence to self-direction (or independence), experience gathered during one's life becomes an invaluable resource for further knowledge acquisition, and cultivation of these increases one's orientation so information is applicable to real-life scenarios in which the adult can immediately apply concepts. Having established these principles, Knowles acknowledges that adults need to oversee the planning, evaluating, experiencing, and determining the relevancy and impact of a lesson on one's life (Pappas, 2013).

While some might argue that both pedagogy and andragogy are the same, we differ. The following example may be helpful. We remember one Sunday morning when a pastor said, "This is how you should think about ____." We looked at one another and laughed, saying, "We're adults. We know how to think." Yet amid the amusement is something more disturbing. We're not sure if the pastor was trying to tell us what to believe or was using his words to gather our attention. We're adult learners. In a children's class, with the use of pedagogy, we might say, "Children, here's how to do this. Here's what you should know." But we're not children, are we? It might be that church leaders start with the assumption that some people are less knowledgeable about the Bible or theology, or that they need direct advice. While that may be true, they're adults trying to acquire skills, and that's not how adults learn. It's like the adage, "Give a man [woman] a fish and he [she] eats for a day. Teach a man [woman] to fish, and he [she] eats for a lifetime." Our goal is for adults to apply lessons in their homes, their work, and their purpose in living.

We believe there is confusion in our churches about what it means to offer adult teaching moments, making assumptions that people need specific directions on how to believe, rather than inviting or demonstrating to them how to think so they can acquire conviction that carries them through the most difficult times. The best statement we ever heard from a minister was this: "I'm not here to feed you. I'm here to make you thirsty." We wanted to stand and applaud this. Yes, this is what we mean. Jesus doesn't offer banalities. Instead, he tells familiar stories of the day and adds a unique twist and then poses a provocative question.

Another common mishap is the assumption that adults magically evolve by listening to someone speak or reading a lesson. If the church desires for believers to become change agents in the world, then it must find a way to encourage and model that worldview. To do so, we need to create an environment conducive to self-reflection and integration. Leaders need to use imagination to redefine problems and generate innovative solutions and develop a place free from coercion where people receive respect, are heard, where their past experiences are valued, as well as have equal opportunity to express opinions and influence church direction. Rather than shutting people down through passive listening or ignoring conflicting beliefs, the church ought to value the diversity of thought, provide empathy for other perspectives, and seek out the commonalities or, at least, find ways to respect all points of view. In his theory, Mezirow says,

> To promote discovery learning, the educator often reframes learner questions in terms of the learner's current level of understanding . . .the key idea is to help the learners actively engage the concepts presented in the context of their own lives and collectively critically assess the justification of new knowledge (1997, p. 10).

To do so means that teachers must resign as sole authorities on the subject matter and instead assume the roles of provocative agents and group facilitators. When we make people think more deeply, they walk away reflecting throughout the week, and that's when the church lesson becomes transformative. It is being lived out daily as people try to make sense of what they heard and how it fits their understanding of God. Plus, it demonstrates that we trust the Divine One to work within adults to lead them in a deeper spiritual walk.

It is concerning when we focus on providing people with information rather than engaging them in revising their core beliefs about themselves, others, and the world. It seems to be a standard error in churches. We preach about repentance, reconciliation, and renewed lives, but we are not adept at showing people how to change from the inside out. As Byrd suggests, "While transformative learning has been found to be an important, if not essential aspect of significant religious growth and change, there has been little work done in developing a method of promoting or assisting such religious transformative change" (2011, p. 251). This type of metamorphosis occurs with a structural shift in how we think, feel, and act. It's a permanent alteration in how we imagine life, how we relate to others, and how we conceptualize God. Isn't it time to do this?

Mistakes in Training

Churches have difficulty in recruiting volunteers to lead groups and, as a result, offer little to no training for those people. This is understandable but we must be clear about our purposes in offering adult education. We desire that Christians receive high quality lessons that bring about inner and outer transformation. In order to accomplish this, we must recruit teachers who have the motivation, commitment, and disposition to teach adults, and then must offer training and support.

However, we notice some common mistakes in this area.

If we assume that adults just need to listen and absorb, then likely we will recruit those leaders who echo the status quo referendum. However, if our goal is to change lives, then we need teachers with a sense of calling and who are committed to adult theories and methods. We observe that many volunteers have no understanding or no commitment to learning these theories and simply rely upon proclamation and regurgitation. Rarely do we hear of teachers speaking of God's calling to lead adults.

We notice that teachers who have little to no training rely upon impartation of information. While this approach is readily adapted, it does not honor adult learning processes, nor does it fit contemporary society where information arrives instantaneously, and where attention spans are short. These factors challenge the instructor to find new ways to engage the adult learner. Even the American Bar Association recognizes the need for updating training for teachers, with a focus on metacognition and self-regulated learning. Faculties are instructed to provide formative responses that give constant and immediate feedback that is useful, as well as allowing for reflection in the classroom (Allen & Jackson, 2017). The church needs to help leaders and teachers in achieving these skills. Perhaps an introduction to teaching workshop is an opportunity for those who desire to teach at church. In a teaching seminar, theories, methodology, and implementation are part of the curriculum, and then on-going support assists in acquiring additional ideas.

Yet another mistake we notice is a lack of preparation. When our parents taught at church, they spent hours looking up scripture, finding commentaries, reading articles, and then fashioning a lesson. We've moved away from teachers doing this and reading a variety of sources to back up their instruction. Instead, many leaders have a guide telling them the scripture, the explanation of the scripture, and even the questions to ask the group. While this makes it easier for teachers, and ensures consistency among classes, if the leader goes no further, then it becomes mere mimicry. Frankly, the lesson becomes dull as the students listen to a lecture in which there is no passion because it is not coming from the original voice and does not invite interaction.

There are times when we look at the instructions and plans and wonder what the course developer is thinking. And there are times when the lesson focuses on the simple and sometimes more mundane reading of the scripture. Forbid that anyone raise issues that are not part of the literature, questions that have no clear answers, or concerns with which even biblical scholars struggle. And if they do, another person in the class may offer clichés, such as, "Well, that's just what the Bible says. If it says it, I believe it." Wait a minute. Did God not give us brains? If we genuinely believe that we are created *imago Dei*, in God's image, and we are bearers of God's characteristics, then that must also mean that we are creative, intelligent, and resourceful humans. As God's creation, we can use those qualities to enrich our understanding of the Holy One so we can shine in a world of darkness. Perhaps we need to take another look at our methods of delivery.

There are classes we find that are using this form of instruction. In some, there are a variety of teachers who bring different ideas and practices to the group. One may bring questions while another brings sensory experiences, and yet another focuses on book studies. The emphasis is on the adults in the group questioning, responding, and testing information. There are times when someone presents an idea to which a participant disagrees, but that is acceptable in this type of setting. A good day is when everyone leaves and carries the lesson throughout the week, attempting to apply what they heard or saw.

Our goal is to encourage those who are currently leading to opt for learning experiences that are well fitted for adults. As we watch, discuss, and pray, we see there is no better example than Jesus. We share our perspective on how Jesus taught, specifically his model of discovery, thereby providing lessons for all of us to disciple others. After all, his words still inspire and draw us to the One who provides redemption and wholeness. The critical test is in the fruit of the one who teaches.

Reflection

Aggravated with us yet? We hope so. We would rather you be stimulated in some way and hope that you are not bored. Let's consider some further questions.

1. We talk about how adults learn in this chapter. Do you agree or disagree? Why or why not?

   _____
   _____
   _____

2. What statement do you find the most challenging? If you could enter discourse with us, what would you want to say?

   _____
   _____
   _____

3. According to some sources, the church is losing adults weekly. Tell us why.

   _____
   _____
   _____

PART II
A DIFFERENT WAY

"What do you want me to do for you" (Mk. 10:51)?

Sarah stopped coming to our class. We wondered what happened and called her up even though we were not the people in charge. We were concerned for her and expressed that. While she was appreciative of our inquiry, Sarah told us she didn't feel like she fit in. "I'm a square peg in a round hole," she said. As we invited her to share more, she let us know that she was looking for a group that was interested in hearing her thoughts rather than telling her what her beliefs should be. "I've worked through a lot of issues to get myself to the place where I'm comfortable with myself and what I believe. Sometimes I don't agree with the statements, but I don't feel the freedom to say that in the class." Sarah's honesty amazed and saddened us at the same time. We hope the group is a safe place for people to come and share their heartfelt concerns, experiences, and hopes. Instead, Sarah chose to continue her spiritual growth in isolation. That concerns us because we believe that spiritual formation best occurs in the context of community. We wonder how we can change the system to ensure the class is a welcoming place for anyone who attends.

During this time, we realized that we had the perfect perspective of teaching right in front of us – Jesus. If we could train our teachers to develop a theory of teaching like Jesus and if they could adopt Jesus' approaches, then we would have an atmosphere that allowed for spiritual formation. We knew this needed to be a place where people were free from judgment, able to be vulnerable, share their deepest sorrows and doubts, and their greatest joys. We also knew that adults needed creative ways to listen and explore, even though that might lead them down diverse paths. We wanted any disagreement to be acceptable as people re-worked their belief systems. Our experiences in the best learning environments and our passion for adult spiritual formation led us to envision a different way to teach spiritual formation to adults.

CHAPTER 3
DISCOVERY IN TEACHING

"As was his custom, he taught them" (Mark 10:1)

When we look at Jesus' teaching, we see some things that help us in our theory development and the subsequent methods. We're not talking about the times when Jesus is speaking to large groups of people. Those times necessitate a different style of oration. When we refer to his style of training, we mean how Jesus interacts one on one or in small groups like his disciples. Those become the exemplary teaching paradigm for growth or community groups. With these people, he communicates with a purpose, trusting that those who are receptive will respond accordingly; his time is spent telling a story, sometimes re-telling a well-known story but adding a different ending. He intentionally refuses to answer some questions and instead chooses to respond with provocative questions that create an atmosphere in which the listener can contemplate the meaning. Jesus encourages deliberation and refuses to provide superficial responses. He fashions unforgettable experiences for those groups and finally sends them out to practice what they learn. All these things make his instruction outstanding so that the lessons reverberate today.

Jesus continually intermingles with his listeners. He relates to them on a personal level, and that allows his followers to respect him and desire to learn from him. A theory of learning must first determine how adults change. After all, that's our goal, isn't it? We believe the aim is to lead adults into life-altering experiences that inform them at every level, whether at work, play, in relationships, and with God. Manternach says,

> In the practice of teaching one engages others in reflective and critical thinking about their lives in light of the gospel tradition. Teachers have a role to nurture and appropriately challenge both individuals and communities in appropriating the tradition and making conscious decisions to live their faith (2002, p. 275).

As we talk about how Jesus teaches, we realize we need to help leaders impart lessons in this same manner. Dr. HeeKap Lee discusses all the facets of teaching to which we refer, including the differences between discovery teaching and exposition-based teaching. He explains that discovery teaching emphasizes the inductive reasoning process while focusing on concepts or relationships. In this modus of learning, the participant uses his or her mind rather than merely accepting an explanation from an authority, thus constructing the meaning and then being altered in the process as the learner seeks to apply what they learn (Lee, 2006). In contrast, exposition-based teaching is where someone presents materials in a complete form, using deductive reasoning (Lee, 2006), and that represents the majority of instruction that we espy in religious settings. Discovery teaching summarizes our beliefs about the teaching of Jesus.

According to this model, the goal is to lead the student to hear the lesson or read the Bible, creating new hypotheses to apply and own the knowledge. It happens as a result of a leader's ability to provide the type of learning environment, creative experiences, and critical questions to inspire students at teachable moments (Lee, 2006). This is the type of lesson that endures long after the teacher departs. It involves the learner taking an active part in his or her acquisition of knowledge and thus becomes the catalyst that modifies worldviews. Lee says, "Jesus was interested in changing mindsets, not just outward behaviors" (2006, p. 3). So how does Jesus accomplish this goal of converting worldviews? As we explore the scriptures, we notice that Jesus employs specific techniques, such as creating teachable moments, employing powerful narratives, sparking curiosity, and allowing reflection, to motivate and inspire or evoke responses.

Create Teachable Moments

So how does Jesus create teachable moments with adult individuals and groups? First, he identifies instances when these people are accessible and open. Ever notice how many times

Jesus says, "He who has ears to hear?" Some say that Jesus is trying to get the attention of his listeners. We propose that Jesus is alluring people to go deeper, hinting that there is an unexplored meaning to his words. The statement is stimulating, indicating that perhaps some people are not listening. We believe that people listen at different levels. Some people understand what they want to hear, which fits into their frame of reference. Others hear the words and filter the information through life experiences, sometimes distorting the story. Think of the many times when the news is passed around and eventually changes until the ending narrative is nowhere close to the original story. Other people listen and re-tell a fable that suits them, which often happens in the context of disagreement. We tell people, the truth is a three-story house: your story, their story, and the real story. Others can listen with more discernment of the underlying question or meaning. These are the moments to which we refer. We believe Jesus is calling listeners to a deeper awareness of profound truth, and they need to discover this lesson in their own time. So, our first lesson about teaching is identifying or creating an environment that allows for teachable moments.

There's a saying, "When the student is ready, the teacher will appear." Jesus understands when his followers are ready for teaching and he uses the opportunity to introduce a lesson. Throughout the Gospels, Jesus is active. He walks from town to town, fishes with his disciples, and sits down to eat with people. In all of these, Jesus seeks out the ones who are willing to learn and then follows through with his strategy. Remember wee little

Zacchaeus? He is the short man who climbs up a sycamore tree to gain a better view of Jesus (Lk. 19:1-10). Zacchaeus is not unnoticed by Jesus, who discerns the tax collector's readiness to listen and respond. And recall the woman with the issue of blood who touches the hem of Jesus' cloak? Jesus says, "Who touched me" (Lk. 8:45)? Jesus uses this moment to speak truth and healing into this woman's life. In Matthew 16:18, when Jesus questions his disciples about what men are saying about him and Simon responds that Jesus is the Messiah, Jesus replies, "And I tell you that you are Peter, and on this rock I will build my church, and the gates of hell will not overcome it." Wow, doesn't that leave Simon Peter wondering what Jesus means? These become unforgettable, life-changing moments, not only for individuals but also for those observing. They are not inconsequential transactions but are tucked away in the memories of the Gospel writers.

Employ Powerful Narratives

Telling stories is part of being human. Go into any café or convenience store or barbershop, and you will find someone telling an anecdote. We listen to stories every day. Some we remember for a short time, and others impress us, and we pass that tale on to others. Social networks are a form of storytelling. Whether in tweets, posts, or photos, we have an innate desire to tell our narrative and to have it heard by others. Stories make us feel alive. We attend movies, watch live stream webinars, or even record television series to feel a sense of connection to something bigger than ourselves. Potent stories point out universal struggles and truths for all of us. Storytelling is typical in every culture of the world (Lawrence & Paige, 2016).

It is no surprise, then, that Jesus uses parables to communicate with us. At least one-third of Jesus' words recorded were parables (Snodgrass, 2008). The parables of Jesus are primarily about the kingdom of God. The parables provide an understanding and expectation for us in how to relate to God and one another. Rabbis commonly use parables as a form of indirect communication. "Rabbis spoke of parables as handles for understanding Torah; before parables, no one understood the Torah, but when Solomon and others created parables, then people understood" (Snodgrass, 2008, p. 8). In his parables, Jesus is intentionally providing a window into an understanding of God. They are strong messages that continue to demand examination and from which new lessons arise with each re-telling or re-reading. At times they are intentionally abstruse while sometimes they are clear in meaning. The goal is to change people; Jesus offers stories that help us see life at different levels. While a parable might have a practical significance for everyday living, it also has a more substantial meaning (Snodgrass, 2008). This approach is what makes the stories lasting and why instructors need to learn how to tell or use a good story.

Madeleine Boucher (1981) explains the types of parables that Jesus teaches: similitude, parable, and exemplary story. The similitude is the most concise, usually occurring in the present tense. Examples of Jesus' similitude parables include the lost coin (Lk 15:8-10) or the growing seed (Mk. 4:26-29). Other times,

Jesus begins the parable by setting up a comparative analysis when he asks, "Which of you?" These brief allegories alert the audience and arouse their curiosity. Notice how short these are. There are times when all of us give too many details, and the observer becomes lost or disinterested. In her book, *Jesus, CEO,* Laurie Beth Jones notes this characteristic about Jesus and remarks that her friend, Sally Scaman says, "Be bold, be brief, be gone" (as cited in Jones, 1995, p. 115).

In the extended parable, the story is fantasy. It is not something occurring in the present or past. Examples of these include the sower and the seed (Mt. 13:3) and the persistent widow (Lk. 18:1-8). Jesus tells them in such a way that sparks the interest of his listeners and leaves them wanting to hear more. The practice of developing passionate fiction and the use of dramatic performance engage adults.

In the exemplary story, Jesus provides specific examples to illustrate moral behavior. Such stories are the Good Samaritan (Lk. 10:29-37) or the Pharisee and the tax collector (Lk. 18:9-14). Jesus uses these less often to illustrate general principles, usually demonstrating the difference between honorable and dishonest characters. No matter what type of parable Jesus tells, there is something about how Jesus brings the story to life that captures the attention of those around him. Knowing how to present narratives is a skill worth learning.

Spark Curiosity

Mystery, provocative statements, and difficult questions are part of Jesus' discovery teaching. He asks questions that make people think. Remember the woman at the well? Jesus first elicits a favor, "Give me a drink." Jesus knows that she's a Samaritan and that a Jew wouldn't ask for water. Why does he do that? He wants her attention, which he gets. But that isn't enough because when she tells him he shouldn't be asking her for a drink, he makes another provocative statement. "If you knew the gift of God, and who it is that is saying to you, 'Give me a drink,' you would have asked him, and he would have given you living water" (Jn. 4:10). But that's not even enough. Jesus makes five more provoking statements to this woman, ultimately leading her to believe in him, followed by her testimony to her people of the one who told her the truth. John 4:39 tells the reader that many Samaritans from that town came to believe because of this woman's witness, and they ask Jesus to stay for several days, resulting in more believers. Think what may have happened if Jesus merely preached at the woman or dismissed her when she first refuses to give him a drink. Instead, he creates a memorable experience that changes her life. The lesson for us is to refrain from lecturing and instead offer truth in a language that inspires learning. He led her into wanting more by initially withholding information and developing a sense of mystery.

At other times, Jesus asks confrontational questions. Remember Nicodemus? Jesus already has the Pharisee's attention because he sought Jesus at nighttime. Why at night? Perhaps he came after hearing Jesus, or to meet with Jesus privately in the darkness of night. Who knows? But he comes as one who is interested and tells Jesus that he knows Jesus comes from God. Once again, Jesus starts with a stimulating statement, but when Nicodemus asks, "How can this be," Jesus replies with a challenging question. "You are Israel's teacher and do you not understand these things" (Jn. 3:10)? That's almost an insulting question. Ever have anyone question your credibility or experience? But Jesus doesn't stop there. Instead, he asks another intriguing question in v. 12, "I have spoken to you of earthly things and you do not believe; how then will you believe if I speak of heavenly things?" Why would he do this? He is trying to help the Pharisee move from an acknowledgment that Jesus is a *good teacher* from God to the conviction that Jesus is the *son* of God come to bring light to the world, meaning the Messiah. Is this too much for Nicodemus? Remember that Nicodemus was a ruler of the Pharisees, a dominant position. Did Nicodemus believe? That's hard to know, but we do know that after Jesus' death, Nicodemus comes with Joseph of Arimathea to prepare Jesus' body for burial (John 19:39).

Notice the times when Jesus asks, "Do you understand?" (Mt. 13:51; Mt. 15:16; Mt. 16:8; Mk. 7:18; Mk. 4:13; Mk. 8:17; Jn. 10:6; Jn. 8:43). This question engages the hearer's cognitive and spiritual perception, which results in obedience to God. It activates an acceptance of God's revelation and moves on to a relationship with God that produces true knowledge (Lee, 2019, personal communication). The question probes and prompts listeners to think and take action.

Another way that Jesus teaches in the discovery manner is to turn things upside down by declaring opposition to an accepted truth. In Matthew 5, Jesus says six times, "You have heard it said…But I say." The first is about murder, then adultery, divorce, taking oaths, revenge, and enemies. He takes a common truth and adds a different ending. In this way, Jesus is challenging the status quo. Remember those Pharisees? They are the religious professors and the Jewish authority of the culture. Yet, Jesus unabashedly criticizes them openly, often saying, "Woe to you." Eight times in Matthew, he warns them because their practices do not match their words. They teach God but not love, their religion is dead, and they are hypocritical. It is shocking to hear Jesus so directly speak against them. Perhaps this is a lesson for all of us to be unafraid to declare truth despite opposition.

The Pharisees struggle with hypocrisy; therefore, Jesus frequently confronts them. Jesus is changing the rules of the game. He takes long-held interpretations of scriptures and stories and presents a different way of thinking about these. Even as a young boy, Jesus was questioning the theology of his elders when his parents find him in the temple sitting with the rabbis asking questions (Luke 2:46-47). In this way, Jesus uses controversy to destabilize those around him so they will search for discernment.

Allow Reflection

Jesus encourages and allows time for reflection. Look at the characteristics of his teaching. He uses multiple ways of representations, inquiry-based strategies, real-life connections, and formative inquiry (checking for understanding), and opportunities for application and evaluation (Lee, 2019, personal communication). He does this through literary devices such as offering an enigma when he curses the fig tree in Matthew 21:19, or hyperbole when Jesus says to cut off one's right hand if it causes you to sin (Mt. 5:30), or paradox when he calls us to take God's yoke to find rest (Mt. 11:29). At other times, Jesus uses puns, jokes, or replaces one word for another. He uses these strategies when he refers to the Pharisees. Unfortunately, the written translation loses the humor (Gagliardi). Through these devices, Jesus is showing his followers that some lessons come through reflection. He addresses issues of murder, adultery, love, revenge, and prejudice, hoping that his disciples will think about these and form new thoughts and take action.

Reflective practice requires time. One example occurs when the woman is caught in adultery (Jn. 8:1-11). One can marvel why Jesus hesitates at the question, "'Teacher, this woman has been caught in the act of adultery. Now in the law Moses commanded us to stone such. What do you say about her'" (v. 4-5)? Jesus draws in the sand. We can speculate about what he's drawing or writing, but the more important aspect is that Jesus allows time for introspection. Not that Jesus desires it but instead those who ask the question need it. Silence often increases vulnerability as people await a response. And that position is precisely where Jesus wants the crowd before he responds, "Okay, so any of you who have not sinned can cast the first stone." This reticence demonstrates its usefulness; it requires knowing how and when to bring pause, silence, and an opportunity to think about the dilemma.

Throughout conversations with his followers, Jesus shows them how to construct new meanings by focusing on ideas and relationships rather than facts and the law. This is what we want for our adult learners! Dr. Lee (2019) says, "Education should provide the basis for enhanced understanding of the world which can be expected to yield higher engagement, more active use and transfer of knowledge, and indeed better retention of knowledge." Jesus captures the attention of his listeners and then wisely chooses the words, the story, the question, or the moment to lead them into the discovery of a new life. Most of Jesus' words move across Bloom's taxonomy, calling people to recall, evaluate, analyze, synthesize, and apply the lessons (Lee & Roso, 2010). This is the mode of teaching we need in churches.

Reflection

This chapter focused on some of the elements we believe are important in teaching adults.

1. We talked about teachable moments, powerful narratives, mysteries, provocative statements, conflict, reflection, and making memories. Of these elements, which have you found most helpful in your spiritual formation?

   _____
   _____
   _____

2. Which of the above elements do you find less helpful, or less interesting?

   _____
   _____
   _____

3. If you could have a conversation with your current teacher/leader, which of the elements would you ask them to include more of in their lessons and why?

   _____
   _____
   _____

PART III
TRY THIS INSTEAD

"Why don't you judge for yourselves what is right" (Lk. 12:57)?

Teaching adults can be rewarding, but it can also present some challenges. The competition with short attention spans, technology, instantaneous communication, and open access to resources creates a dilemma for even the most qualified facilitator. It is vital that those who disciple others intentionally examine their belief system and develop a sound theory of spiritual formation development. The leader chooses techniques carefully and purposefully, and allows space for the free flow of thoughts in a group. Then the teacher can guide adults to a meaningful experience. Rather than viewing one's self as the wise teacher with expertise in the Bible, the leader best facilitates spiritual growth through skillful collaboration with the learners.

The group dynamics are a crucial element in the teaching process. One must recognize the communication style and the power dynamics while focusing on both the whole class as well as individual members. Annobil and Thompson say,

> Teaching is a process by which one interacts with another person with the intention of influencing the learning of that person. It is the interplay between the teacher and the learners. Teaching, as a useful and practical art, calls for intuition, creativity, improvisation and expressiveness. Teaching methods are those strategies which a teacher uses to effect learning (Annobil & Thompson, 2017, p. 319).

Methodology becomes a central focus and we consider how Jesus uses various techniques to accomplish his purposes. In reviewing scripture, we quickly find that Jesus creates teachable moments, employs powerful narratives, sparks their curiosity, and makes them think.

CHAPTER 4
CREATE TEACHABLE MOMENTS

*"Which of you fathers, if your son asks for a fish,
will give him a snake instead" (Lk. 11:11)?*

Every day brings opportunities for growing closer to Christ. Most often, these occasions occur at times when the adult is receptive to hearing and changing. Jesus does not hold conferences or regular meetings. Instead, he interacts with people daily and presents ideas that are relevant to their personal life and brings them closer to God. He uses whatever occasion arises, and it makes his teaching vibrant. For example, in Matthew 12:1-8, Jesus and his disciples become hungry and decide to pick grains to eat on the Sabbath. The Pharisees rebuke him, but Jesus seizes the moment to ask a question:

> "Haven't you read about David?" [Notice the irony.] "When he was hungry? He entered God's house and ate from there. He ate the priest's meal! Or didn't you read in the Law" [another moment of being facetious], "that on the Sabbath,

the priests slaughter the sacrifice and eat it and yet you don't accuse them of breaking the Law?" Jesus doesn't stop there but proclaims that one greater than the temple is here (Matt. 12:41).

And in verse 8, Jesus delivers the coup de grâce when he says, "For the Son of man is Lord of the Sabbath…The Sabbath was made for man [woman], and not man [woman] for the Sabbath: so that the Son of man is Lord even of the Sabbath." Don't be confused. Jesus does not mistake that the Pharisees are approachable but rather that this is a chance for his disciples to absorb several observations about the Pharisees, the Law, the kingdom of God, and Jesus' identity. The disciples grew up knowing and obeying the law, if they were faithful Jewish followers, and thus choosing to pick and eat on the Sabbath, and then hearing how Jesus responds to the Jewish rulers demonstrates there is a new lesson for them.

For Jesus to recognize the times when people are most open, he must remain in touch with their emotional, spiritual, and physical needs. Whether it is the recognition of hunger, and then feeding 5,000 men and their families from five barley loaves and two small fish (Mt. 14:13-21), or on a ship that is dangerously rocking during a storm (Mk. 4:35-41), or turning water into wine at a wedding (Jn. 2:1-11), Jesus is sensing the need of those around him. Notice that Jesus doesn't *immediately* meet the needs before people request something from him. He lets individuals struggle with their fear and anxiety. Jesus allows their discomfort knowing that during distress comes the willingness to learn. Roberto and Minkiewicz say, "While transmitting knowledge is important, it is not the primary role of the teacher of adults. Teachers create space for adults to find their own voice as Christian learners and Christian knowers" (2007, p. 9). There are other ways of helping people incorporate the lessons. In the examples provided, Jesus lets people grapple with problems and then acts benevolently without preaching. In this way, the modality becomes an object lesson that demonstrates faith and requires the observers to interpret, synthesize, and apply the message.

Adults learn during pivotal times, such as life transitions that question past and present constructions of meaning. The best teachers understand that adults have developmental phases that demand changes (Roberto & Minkiewicz, 2007). By letting adults experience the growth process that naturally occurs, and being aware of how those passages impact adults, the skilled teacher snatches the instant to allow the strife while offering support. This requires the leader pay careful attention to the lives of those whom one is teaching. What are they talking about? What most concerns them? What dilemmas are they facing? How are they making meaning of their current circumstance, or are they confused, or in despair? Through prayer requests and casual conversations before and after meetings, the watchful teacher tucks these away to fashion lessons that address these concerns.

Other periods when adults are amenable to learning occur when they become stuck, and the former answers are no longer enough, or the adults become aware that they need additional knowledge (Easterday, 2016). This chance may occur during times of loss, or when adults are in survival mode or face discouragement. These storms may bring disappointment with God or the church, or doubts about one's faith. Paul Tournier says, "Where there is no longer any opportunity for doubt, there is no opportunity for faith either" (as cited in Yancey, 1998). More often we want to make people feel better, and so we offer advice or tell them we will pray for them, or buy a card. We let *our* anxiety about their dilemma short circuit their need to uncover new veracities. And while those come with good intentions, that is not how God treats us in those moments. Instead, God allows us to sit in our rough state, sometimes responding later, and sometimes not at all.

When we read the story of Job, it is important to notice that God does not respond to Job's inquiries until chapter 38. For the first 37 chapters of the book, however long that time may be, God is silent. We know that it is at least a week, for Job's friends sit with him for seven days and seven nights (Job 2:13), and so it's likely months before God answers Job's accusations. Perhaps we need to learn to sit quietly beside one another before trying to speak; for in those silences, the lesson may unfold. This integration can only occur if the teacher is less concerned about conveying knowledge and more attuned to the spiritual development of adults. During these times, the leader may need to identify the type of spiritual distress students are experiencing. According to NANDA International (formerly the North American Nursing Diagnosis Association), spiritual distress is "impaired ability to experience and integrate meaning and purpose in life through connectedness with self, others, art, music, literature, nature, and/or a power greater than oneself" (as cited in Chaves, de Carvalho, Beijo, Goyata, & Pillon, 2011, p. 903). Dr. Rudolf Klimes, a former professor at Harvard University, spoke of several manifestations of spiritual distress: pain, alienation, anxiety, guilt, anger, loss, and despair. Determining the type of suffering can guide the instructor in knowing what kind of teaching intervention these adults need. We must not underestimate the power of these precipitous periods to lead others to higher levels of spirituality.

While the previously mentioned times occur as a result of life events, they leave us with little control over the timing. Is it possible to create teachable moments? The answer is obvious. Of course, we can. So how can the astute leader do so? We once watched a movie wherein the protagonist continually stated, "There are signs everywhere." Perception is critical in snatching opportunities that are conducive to learning. Too often we desire for things to go smoothly and orderly. However, it is in the moments that things do not go well that open the door for novel possibilities. Simple mishaps, such as a loss of technology or absence of the scheduled speaker, are openings for fresh insights and often lead to conversations in a group that become quite profitable for growth. When conflicts occur, they present a chance to use the disagreement as a learning tool. If the leader has developed a safe environment, then that frees both the leader and participants to take risks, which in turn can result in fascinating discoveries. All of this requires that teachers be on the lookout for these moments.

Another way to think of teachable moments comes from the concept of "thin places." The idea of thin places comes from the Celtics. People describe these as a place where heaven and earth meet, a sacred spot where one "catches glimpses of the divine" (Weiner, 2012). These locales are where spiritual breakthroughs occur. In the scripture, examples of such places might be Mt. Sinai, the temple, or the Garden of Gethsemane.

And yet, it's not simply the location but rather the time in which a person feels closer to God and so we must not think of spiritual formation as limited to a specific setting, like the church. Thin moments occur in sacred experiences. They may be when the community group serves in a non-profit setting, such as a shelter, or in building a home for someone, or in caring for a member who is ill or grieving, or perhaps during communion. Sacred interludes occur when we see things more clearly, or maybe uniquely. Paul MacCormack describes it:

> Thin moments are essentially those experiences when we feel in our bones that we are part of something much larger than what our everyday thought processes dictate. Our notions of self disappear briefly, and we become present to the moment as it unfolds before us; an expanded form of conscious awareness (2013, para. 4).

A thin moment occurs at the burning bush. Out of his inquisitiveness, Moses goes to look at that bush, and God says, "Do not come any closer. Take off your sandals, for the place where you are standing is holy ground" (Exodus 3:5). Now is the ground holy, or is it that the occasion is holy because the Lord is present? The Lord is always present with us, and if we are listening and looking for Him, the event can also be holy.

Teachers can generate these by listening, attending, inviting, and providing a worshipful place for students. One such moment occurred recently in our community group when we brought a singing bowl to class. We did a *Lectio Divina*, which is a scriptural reading combined with prayerful meditation. We read the scripture three times, using a singing bowl between readings. Each time we asked the class to focus on something different: a meaningful word, a feeling, and a message received. The sharing of this experience was a useful reflection on God's word for the day and touched each person. Using variety in teaching approaches encourages the exploration of spiritual messages in different ways.

Teachable moments, planned or unplanned, generate what Beard refers to as a "kairos" moment, meaning a lesson or observation that occurs during times when students are personally or communally disoriented. It may be a current event, a life change, or an effect composed by the instructor. These moments become synergistic as they allow for critical reflection and reconstruction of one's beliefs (Breen, 2015). Discovery teaching like Jesus necessitates finding teachable moments.

Reflection

Ever have moments that have been the best learning experiences? Did you feel like the time or place was right? How about a moment that felt truly sacred when you were most aware of God's presence? Tell us about these.

1. The best learning experience in my spiritual journey was?

    _____
    _____
    _____

2. The place(s) or time(s) that have been most sacred to me were?

    _____
    _____
    _____

3. I was most aware of God's presence in my life when? What can I do to re-experience that?

    _____
    _____
    _____

CHAPTER 5
EMPLOY POWERFUL NARRATIVES

"What shall I compare the kingdom of God to" (Lk. 13:20)?

Ever know someone who was a great storyteller? Perhaps you may not remember who it was, but you probably recall the story. The best literature pulls us in and then becomes enduring. Think of novels written that are unforgettable: *The Odyssey* (Homer, 8th century BC), *Hamlet* (William Shakespeare, 1603), *Pride and Prejudice* (Jane Austen, 1813), *Frankenstein* (Mary Shelley, 1818), *Moby Dick* (Herman Melville, 1851), *Les Misérables* (Victor Hugo, 1862), *Crime and Punishment* (Fyodor Dostoyevsky, 1866), and *Animal Farm* (George Orwell, 1945). These stories are told and re-told. They are made into movies and become the basis for other stories. They entice us into the drama and portray our lives, trials, and relationships while exploring our mistakes, character defaults, and our triumph over calamities, difficulties, social injustice, and evil.

Jesus is a master storyteller. He knows to capture the attention of his audience and convey a story that connects with his listeners' concerns, hopes, and dreams in daily life. His stories are known even among those who are not religious. Most people are familiar with The Good Samaritan or The Prodigal Son. While he never took high school literature, he knows that every good story requires a protagonist, antagonist, and a conflict. Whether he tells of the unforgiving servant, the lost coin, or the ten virgins, the drama compels the hearer to question, to re-enact, or to further explore the hidden meaning. The stories are brief. They don't go into a long chronology. Instead, Jesus focuses on the salient points where some alteration occurs. His messages teach about the world, God, and human character. They center on issues of justice and the kingdom of God. One does not hear the stories of Jesus and walk away unmoved. The lesson remains within, digging deep like a perennial seed planted in fertile ground, growing unseen until one must notice it, choosing to weed it or allow it to bloom into fullness.

So, it is with the skillful teacher. The use of narrative in teaching adults is an essential tool for learning. Espinoza says, "When we tell stories as part of our teaching, we invite people to enter a world that may be different from their own, but remarkably similar in many ways" (2013, p. 433). Narratives shape personal and community identity. They show us who we are, to what we belong, and how we ought to be. "They build familiarity and trust, allowing listeners to enter the story from where the hearer is in life and creates an openness to learning:

(Lee, 2019, personal communication). Stories are the process by which character forms. Hampton tells us that narrative shapes sociological norms, serving as a "mirror" by revealing true morality, and assisting us in formulating a paradigm for future spiritual development (Hampton, 2016).

Christians grow in faith by hearing the story of God, the Christian narrative, and then finding a way to re-interpret their lives in the context of that metanarrative (Foote, 2015). The best fiction engenders identification. Jagerson states,

> As the story develops over narrative time, the audience is meant to deeply identify with the characters, their choices, and the consequences of those choices in the midst of the competing needs and desires that arise in the complexities of life (2014, p. 264).

The power of the narrative comes alive when it causes people to ask: what is the meaning and purpose of life? How does my story fit within the grand narrative of scripture and in what way does that empower me to be an agent of change in the world?

Think of the last testimony you heard which touched your heart. You probably have little difficulty remembering it. In scripture, many times over, we hear of lives that change. Like when Abram becomes Abraham, the little shepherd boy David slays the giant Goliath and then becomes king, how Peter moves from betrayal to courageous preacher in Acts, and how John Mark moves from the least favored to writing the first gospel. Our testimonies of faith are commanding. You know you've heard a good story when you can relate to it or when it changes how you view yourself, others, or the world around you. It's an account worth remembering when your heart leaps, and the truth comes alive.

These things transpire when our personal story integrates with God's story. This rewrite of narrative only happens when we surrender our chapter to God, allowing God to take the pen to add to our books, producing the ending where God desires to take us (Lavender, 2014). This is the beauty of spiritual formation: editing our personal narrative into the story of redemption. It moves from a place of despair and questioning one's place in the world to participate in the drama of universal history. As we place ourselves within the larger story of redemption, we come to realize that we have chapters that are turned one page at a time, and that the end of our novel has not yet occurred. And while we do not yet know the finish, we are reassured that the culmination of God's unfolding play results in victory.

It is in this context that the shrewd teacher functions through speaking of redemption while providing a sacred holding place where everyone is free to share their past blunders, their faults, their bitterness, their wounds, their joys, and their desires. Acceptance and compassion is the key. Good teachers know when to confront and when to be gentle, but always allow everyone to express their thoughts.

Rather than trying to hurry a person on while they express a memory or scrapple with a concept, the instructor welcomes the interruption, skillfully guiding the student to completion, so that the lessons from that story may enlighten others. The objective moves from teaching a prescribed study to inhabiting a life lesson. Too often, we see teachers passively listen to a participant and then move quickly to complete their prepared curriculum in the last five minutes, unaware that the group has not shifted from the vulnerable person to the teacher's final departing words. The momentum of the narrative is lost in a rush to accomplish an objective that lies outside of the living story.

The current pace of our world, along with the rapid production of information, produces a dichotomous world in which we are unable to connect with others deeply. We are in a hurry to move from point A to point Z, skipping points B, C, and D. No wonder so many of us deal with anxiety and depression! Is there no one willing to be our witness? That is one of the purposes of the narrative: the sharing of one's story and finding the universality of human strife and celebration of victory amid conflictual circumstances.

It is time for group leaders to learn the skills needed for the development of adult spiritual growth. This follows the example of Jesus. Christ keeps stories simple, short, and relevant. He tells them in such a way that his listeners wonder what he's trying to communicate. He doesn't preach to them. He tells them a story that's easy to remember and sparks their curiosity.

Reflection

If you're still with us, you're doing well. We hope you'll continue on your journey of evaluating your spiritual growth. If you teach adults, then we hope you're gaining some new thoughts about your teaching style.

1. What's the best story you've ever heard? How about the best testimony?

   _____
   _____
   _____

2. What's your favorite story in the Bible? What makes that your favorite?

   _____
   _____
   _____

3. What's one thing you need to change in your teaching style to be more effective with adult learners?

   _____
   _____
   _____

CHAPTER 6
SPARK CURIOSITY

"Why do you call me good" (Lk. 18:19)?

The success of Jesus' teachings often lies in his practices. One such way that he engages his audiences is using mystery, provocative statements, good questions, and controversy. To be sure, it is simpler to make direct statements. However, people often ignore these unless they are command statements directing them where to go or what to do. We hear plenty of these in daily life at work or with our spouse or roommates or some type of authority. It is a type of control talk to elicit cooperation and agreement. However, Jesus is interested in the search for truth and redemption of humans. Thus, his methods become those that utilize activities that require some type of action. His techniques include the use of mystery, provocation, and questioning. He chooses carefully when and where to use each, depending on the people, the context, and the circumstance.

Mystery

We love a good mystery. Whether reading a novel, watching a movie, or even reading the newspaper, we love to solve the "who done it." Notice the popularity of crime shows on television, both fiction and reality-based. The best sorts are those that we think we've solved only to find out in the end that we are wrong. Solving puzzles bring us into the center stage with the actors as we attempt to outwit the bad guys or dissect the clues. There is a feeling of satisfaction in finding the solution.

An important skill in relaying information to adults is the use of mystery. Not knowing where the speaker may go perks the attention of the spectator and places them squarely in the middle of the play. The unpredictability makes it come alive. It would be much simpler to be forthright, but the proclamation would be boring, and the inner and outer distractions of the world might prevent the hearer from gathering what they need. Directness short-circuits the formational goal. Wrapping lessons in allegorical language cloaks the message, resulting in a search for truth one thread at a time.

Jesus does this frequently in talking with others. He says things at times that are not easily understood. Jesus challenges them to reflect on their ways of thinking. Sometimes it occurs in what he doesn't say that produces such a profound effect. For in those moments, as listeners think, they experience that "aha" moment, and the knowledge arises from the heart (Lee, 2019, personal communication). Also, Jesus intrigues his audiences by giving them a puzzling problem or situation. For example, in

John 10 when Jesus is speaking to the Pharisees, he says,

> "Very truly I tell you Pharisees, anyone who does not enter the sheep pen by the gate, but climbs in by some other way, is a thief and a robber. The one who enters by the gate is the shepherd of the sheep. The gatekeeper opens the gate for him, and the sheep listen to his voice. He calls his own sheep by name and leads them out. When he has brought out all his own, he goes on ahead of them, and his sheep follow him because they know his voice." Jesus used this figure of speech, but the Pharisees did not understand what he was telling them (v. 1-6).

When Jesus sees that the Pharisees do not understand, he explains his words, and this results in division among the Jews. Some think Jesus is demon-possessed, or a lunatic, while others disagree. Upon reading the entire passage, one might wonder why the listening Jews respond in such a manner and with such confusion among them. It seems self-explanatory, but is it? In his elucidation, Jesus is stating that God has sent him as the shepherd.

So, what do the listeners not understand? Jesus uses a common metaphor to communicate his message, and the Jews are accustomed to hearing parables, but the meaning of the tale is elusive to the hearers. To understand the muddle, we must remember that the Pharisees and other Jews have no idea who Jesus is at that point. Also, Jesus begins with a rather provocative statement about thieves and robbers. Any listener might wonder,

"What thieves? Who are the robbers?" This makes the interpretation perplexing as Jesus speaks the remainder of the story. Most times, when Jesus speaks of his identity, few understand him, or if they do, they think he is insane. After all, who professes to be God or like God or come from God?

Another example of how Jesus uses mystery in teaching is in Luke 18:31-34. He tells his disciples what is about to happen in Jerusalem, but the disciples do not understand because the meaning is hidden. The words are clear, and in retrospect, it is easy for us to understand because we know the finale, but for those who are walking with Jesus at the time, it makes no sense. Ever meet anyone who said, "I think that something terrible is going to happen to Fred and Pearl. Their son is going to die?" Now, those words are simple, but they are a prediction, and we tend to devalue that which has not yet occurred.

How about in Mark 8 when Jesus feeds the four thousand? The Pharisees come and question Jesus, asking for a sign. Afterward, when his disciples have only one loaf to share, Jesus says, "Be careful. Watch out for the yeast of the Pharisees and that of Herod" (Mk. 8:15). The disciples interpret this literally. When Jesus hears them, he asks, "Why are you talking about bread? Don't you understand? Do you have eyes but fail to see, and ears but fail to hear" (v. 17-18)? Jesus is pointing out that his words have a deeper meaning.

Jesus speaks plainly but also hides a truth within his words. There are times when understanding comes through reflection, or when the time is right, or the student is ready. Speaking in mystery arouses inquisitiveness and leads the learner down a path of exploration. The esoteric messages of Jesus are meant for certain people and not others. Jesus explains this to his disciples in Matthew 13:10-17 when they ask why he speaks in parables. Jesus tells them that his words are for those who can see and hear, not for those who have sight and hearing but refuse to see or hear. The emphasis lies in the motivation of the listener.

Provocative Statements

We entered the class that evening and started it with a jolting statement: "Jesus wasn't a Christian." A look of surprise appeared on their faces and then apprehension. What were we trying to do? Why were we talking negatively about Jesus? One said, "Of course, he was. He was Christ. That makes him a Christian." We continued in the discussion as the adults grappled with the statement we made, finally realizing for themselves that the statement was true. Jesus was a Jew. We simply could have started with that statement, but then the discourse would not have been so rich. It was more important to engage them in their learning process to discover the truth for themselves and what that meant to them.

This is what makes Jesus' teaching so successful. He doesn't use a systematic program. Instead, his teaching is powerful because he connects with people in their current circumstance. Jesus moves beyond explanation of ideas, to the discovery of new solutions and greater possibilities. In the midst of the listener's context, Jesus calls them to respond, and that requires active knowledge construction (Lee, 2019, personal communication).

Provocative statements are a common method that Jesus uses. Think about some of these: "I am the way, and the truth, and the life. No one comes to the Father except through me" (Jn. 14:6). Or how about this one? "If anyone comes to me and does not hate his own father and mother and wife and children and brothers and sisters, yes, and even his own life, he cannot be my disciple" (Lk. 14:26). If that doesn't have your attention, what about Luke 14:27? "Anyone who does not carry his cross and follow me cannot be my disciple." So, go ahead and pick up something used for torture to follow me. Or here is one that will hit you where it hurts. "Go, sell everything you have and give to the poor, and you will have treasure in heaven. Then come, follow me" (Mt. 19:21). Now one can explain all these away. But the impact of these statements initially knocks all of us off-center.

An important concept in learning is how the acquisition of new information is assimilated into present constructs in our minds. Whenever we are faced with some piece of data that does not fit, it creates disequilibrium. Our minds want ideas to fit into our current schema (Piaget, 1985). When notions are discomfiting, we experience tension. Discomfort is a strong motivator for learning. Barrett says, "Used in the correct way, at the correct moment, the right type of provocation creates momentum in our thinking or those around us" (2015, para. 5). Our reactions to provocation manifest as emotional, ideological, cognitive, ethical, or moral challenges. McIntosh says, "The provocation comes at the beginning of learning, along with many other resources and content sources in an immersion that will contradict, delight, frustrate and generate a discord" (2018, para. 18).

One way to motivate adult listeners is to provide something that creates a stir. Perhaps it's a statement, but it might be an image, a video, a quote, music, art, or providing conflicting viewpoints. The objective is to cause people to pause, listen, debate, confront or awaken inner thoughts or doubts, and then to participate in discourse so that their thinking can move to a place of new ideas or solutions.

When people face provocation, they are forced to reconstruct their belief system. For that to occur, they respond initially baffled or defensive, protecting what they fear they may lose if the statement is true. Then in interaction with others, they will seek either an understanding of the assertion or attempt affiliation with their belief system. If the process of learning continues, then they will deconstruct their current knowledge base by examining it closely, meditating and appraising it, and finally move to incorporation or rejection of the new information.

Provocation moves people into vulnerability, and that places them in a position of making decisions about what they will or will not accept. The incendiary statement does not have to be true to be effective. It may be entirely false, but it moves people from a static state to one that is more dynamic. Jesus tends to catch his crowds by surprise by stating something odd, contradictory, unexpected, or arouses curiosity. It is in those moments that he has his listeners exactly where he wants them.

By using the element of surprise, Jesus awakens their desire for more.

Jesus is a troublemaker and uses controversy frequently. He starts causing problems when he is twelve by disappearing from the family camp only to be found asking questions at the temple. Think about his response to his anxious mother, "'Why are you searching for me?' he asked. 'Didn't you know I had to be in my Father's house'" (Lk. 2:49-50)? He offers no apology and little recognition of the worry he causes. We suppose that is typical of most 12-year-old boys, but the child is missing for three days, and he rationalizes his disappearance. Surely Jesus understands the ramifications of his absence in a strange city for such a long time. There are speculations about the meaning of his words, but we believe that the inclusion of this story in Luke's gospel is an introduction to Jesus' oppositional approach and desire to overthrow the status quo. Of all the gospel writers, Luke seems to record more of this attitudinal posture than the others, and it is one of the best techniques to bring about systemic changes. Jesus knew how to heat it up, whether he was talking with his mother, his disciples, his followers, or his critics, and his disciples learn to do this in watching him (Acts 17:6).

Think of the many ways that Jesus behaves and teaches that are countercultural. Jesus rejects the socio-economic principle that wealth brings happiness and power when he states, "Blessed are the poor in spirit, for theirs is the kingdom of heaven" (Mt. 5:3). This challenges how these people view status. It is not something that comes from position, power, or prosperity. Rather, he implies that significance arises from poverty, purity, and potentiality. Chong says,

> Jesus challenges how we look at life – if someone sees himself lacking terms of his ability to do what is right and pleasing to God, and recognizes how desperately he needs God, then this person would surely embrace Jesus' rule in his life [and that makes the person blessed]. When a self-sufficient person thinks he has no need for God, he will not see the value of being in God's kingdom (2018, para. 15).

Wouldn't it be easier for Jesus to come in riches and born with a substantial station in life? His influence could be greater, but that is not how God chooses to bring him into the world.

Another way that Jesus interrupts the entrenched system is through his statements about leadership. In Matthew 20:25-26, he tells his disciples that the person who wants to be the greatest must become the servant. What? Slaves have no voice, no sway, and no vote. Why in the world would anyone desire that role? But Jesus is rejecting the "business as usual" attitude of the current sociopolitical systems. According to Bryant (2017),

> Jesus in a very simplistic way presents a universal message of liberation in the kingdom of God; one that would repeal and replace the oppressive systematic infrastructure. Jesus' message opened the door for the marginalized to have access to and participate in this movement" (p. 156).

There are others for whom Jesus becomes an advocate: those

with leprosy, sinners, the poor, those who are hungry, and women. To each of these, he offers a voice and path to freedom while condemning discriminatory cultural practices.

Even Jesus' parables are subversive. He takes his stories, some that may be common, or have familiar elements and craftily chooses his words so that the references are relevant and yet prod a response or facetiously state a truth. In Mark 12:1-12, Jesus tells the parable of the tenants but ends the story with a quote from Isaiah 5. Those unfamiliar with his use of language, and reading only the interpretation in English, miss his play on words here. The Hebrew words for "son" and "stone" rhyme (Wu, 2015). That would not only capture the listeners' attention but also unsettle them as they wonder who is the son and who is the stone. It is clear that Jesus is referring to the Jewish leaders as the ungrateful tenants. He is presenting them unfavorably, offending the teachers of the law, and resulting in a discussion and plotting of Jesus' arrest.

Jesus' teaching methods follow a frame that consists of three stages: diacognition (providing a certain level of uncertainty and ambiguity), cognition (letting the audience reach that "aha" moment), and recognition (transforming society when the audience applies their learning). Diacognition consists of various layers that provide distinct and yet complementary perspectives that arouse the phenomenology (how we make sense) of the world (Rule, 2017). In this approach, Jesus surreptitiously evokes dialogue, including the intrapersonal, forcing the listener to converse with him or herself; and the interpersonal, inviting responders to converse with one another. From there Jesus invites conversations that include the transpersonal, causing the participant to interact with ideology, culture, or the situation; and ultimately leading his followers to a suprapersonal discourse with God. While dialogue is the beginning, the movement towards transformation continues only when the learner develops intercognition (the ability to recognize the lesson, the 'aha' moment) and metacognition (disorientation and reorientation to a new way of thinking), as well as restructuring his or her position in society and ideology (Rule, 2017). At that point, information moves from an intellectual understanding to a recognition and connection in the heart, and that is what motivates and energizes learners to change. As a result of personal transformation, that excitement leads them out into the world to tell of what they've learned.

Following Jesus' example means that devoted teachers are unafraid to upheave the status quo. To be effective, they move from a polite conversation and impartation of knowledge to suggestions that encourage their participants to question the conventional and move to rebellion if the current system prohibits freedom, inclusion, or acceptance of those who are different. And yet, the humble leader presents him or herself in the posture of a servant. The teacher is not seeking recognition or honor, but rather a place of equity among the members of the group.

The stories or lessons that the teacher presents include intentional language that speaks to those who are present and aims precisely at the lessons necessary for their class. Whether painfully truthful, or facetious, the instructor calls those in the room to participate in the many levels of dialogue, while examining both worldview and status. The teacher reminds those present of Dietrich Bonhoeffer's words (1937), "When Christ calls a man [woman], he bids him [her] come and die." Whether this means that death is literal or figurative, whether it is the demise of one's life, or ideology, becomes the conversation between the listener and the Holy One. And that point is exactly where we want to lead people – into confrontation with God.

Asking Good Questions

Throughout his conversations with individuals and groups, Jesus sparks his audience's curiosity. What is he talking about? What does he mean? To whom is he referring? Why is he saying that? The questions become endless but drive his listeners to explore his statements.

Think about the gospel of John. The first words that Jesus speaks are a question. "What do you seek?" (Jn. 1:38). The last words of Jesus are, "What is it to you?" (Jn. 21:22). And the first words after the resurrection to Mary, "Why are you weeping?" (Jn. 20:15). Is this mere coincidence, or are the questions more meaningful than that? According to Estes (2013), the ancient world was much more accustomed to questions. Consider the study of the Torah and how the Rabbis taught it. They understood the value of and used queries.

Sometimes the questions create disequilibrium, much like provocative statements. "Jesus asked questions to inspire audiences to formulate new schema that challenged their existing framework of ideas" (Lee, 2006, p. 5). Sharp inquiry delivers an opening to re-construct stories, reinforce learning, define truth, and, when used strategically, cause people to refocus so that they can comprehend (Estes, 2013).

In leading groups, we propose that the teacher use this technique rather than trying to lecture or tell people how to think. The key to adult learning is to increase motivation through the inducement of emotional responses to cognitive material. When the two are combined, the lessons explored hold significant value and are less likely forgotten over time.

Sometimes leaders are wary of being misunderstood or misleading people. However, as the participants become familiar and trust the teacher, they learn that this is a device used to open higher levels of thinking. People need to leave groups talking about what occurred in the setting, whether they agree with the statements, and then reflecting on it throughout the week as they attempt to apply or rebuff the statements. This generates a process of learning that is continuous.

Adult spiritual formation should not end when the class is over but continue throughout life. The best experiences, and most treasured, are those that continue to teach us a year, or five years, or twenty years from the present moment. As we recall words, phrases, or unexpected strands of information, we smile with pleasure later at how those become threads in the woven fabric of our theology. The best teachers do not give us a ready-made garment; instead, they provide us with the needle and material to sew together our belief system.

Reflection

Thanks for staying with us. We hope that the cognitive wheels are turning for you. Let's think further about this chapter.

1. Why do you believe it's important to have an element of mystery in your teaching? Think of a time when you used this device or experienced it in a class. What difference did it make for you?

   _____
   _____
   _____

2. Think of the most provocative statement you've ever heard from a leader or teacher, or a statement that you have made to a class. What happened? Was it a success? Why or why not?

   _____
   _____
   _____

3. Good questions are important. In what way can you word or re-word questions to elicit more or a deeper response from your class participants?

   _____
   _____
   _____

CHAPTER 7
MAKE THEM THINK

"What is the kingdom of God like" (Lk. 13: 18)?

Throughout this book, we emphasize the need for contemplation. However, we would be amiss if we do not talk about the many ways in which that can occur. Adults need opportunities to read or hear, acknowledge, question, synthesize, practice, and apply knowledge. The respectable teacher appreciates that learning is an active process and requires activities that include sensory input, interconnection, activation of cognitive processes, and experimental play (Bristol & Isaac, 2009). These are the features that motivate people to explore ontological questions or the reason for human existence, leading them to acceptance of grander purposes concerning the Holy One. All the previous techniques mentioned lead the participant to this penultimate goal of spiritual development.

If we believe that God desires we become instruments of

revolution in a fallen world, then we must confront individual and corporate philosophies that pull people away from God. Jesus says, "Not everyone who says to me, 'Lord, Lord,' will enter the kingdom of heaven, but the one who does the will of my Father who is in heaven" (Mt. 7:21). Jesus' entrance into the world intrudes upon the well-ordered religious world. His statements encourage spiritual leaders and the common man and woman to reconsider the primacy of the Law, the misappropriation of justice, and God's intention for all humankind. He cleverly understands that conversion arises in diverse manners, but in all instances, he must find ways to disrupt the people so they will re-examine the unquestioned worldview.

The process of critical reflection for adult learners is vital to spiritual formation. It is vital that churches clarify the purpose of adult education. Is it for spiritual formation? Or is it for equipping adults with God's words or making a right decision? Or do we teach for the purpose of transforming society? Christians must know and understand why they believe as they do and how that informs their decision-making in their daily lives, whether for small things such as job changes or the broader issues that have political, socioeconomic, or cultural consequences. We have observed in our practices how many believers are linear in their thinking. This does not serve adults well because they have little ability to apply theological or biblical concepts to life problems. Their rigid thinking prevents them from understanding the nuances involved in situational evaluation. They choose what scriptures apply as if they are in the cafeteria line, free to pick what they like or don't like to answer essential questions. For example, when counseling one Christian woman upon separating from her husband of 20 years, she explains that she is now growing closer to God, despite that she has broken a vow to a responsible, caring partner. Huh? Interesting, isn't it? Or when approaching a minister who is fired from his congregation, he responds that they should have appreciated him more, even though he was caught embezzling funds. What?

These illustrations do not demonstrate the spiritual maturity our churches desire for Christians. Neither of the individuals demonstrate the critical thinking to apply biblical principles to problems of life. McKenzie and Harton say,

> There must be room for critical thinking. In too many places, teaching is apprised [sic] as authoritative telling; learning is equated with listening and accepting. The faith-process becomes the receiving of a cultural hand-me-down and not the wrestling with Jacob's angel that leads to authentic commitment (2002, p. 9).

When teachers are more concerned with imparting content, then the data becomes the end target rather than spiritual formation.

Some may doubt that critical reflection is useful or that it might lead a person away from God or the church. We argue that those are people who never had the commitment to begin with and were in denial of the depth of that decision. Critical reflection means using our God-given ability to sort through information, examine it, and reach conclusions before incorporating that into daily practice. "Reflection, then, involves intentionally looking at a situation, an idea, an experience, in order to see what comes back, and then considering the implication of what is seen" (Williams, as cited in Sanders, 2018, p. 91). Critical reflection invites learners to examine their lvies from differing perspectives, drawing them to a logical conclusion, so they can apply new insights to a given situation, and thereby transforming their lives (Lee, 2019, personal communication).

Think about the many ways that Jesus calls his followers to use his lessons. In the Gospels, Jesus poses more than 100 different questions that are practical, rhetorical, provocative, definitive, searching, clarifying, and leading an individual or group to discuss and consider. He uses the parables, poetry, lectures, prayer, apprenticeship, humor, hyperbole, irony, and silence to provide the cognitive room for his listeners to question, analyze, and re-develop their perspectives (Annobil & Thompson, 2017). When we prompt people to practice reflection, we are asking them to examine their underlying assumptions about God, life, and themselves.

In his book, *The Universe Next Door*, James Sire (2009) states that every worldview must answer seven questions. These are questions of theodicy, anthropology, thanatology, epistemology, and ethics, as well as concerns of meaning and purpose and life-long commitments that are consistent with one's response. The questions engage the learner to respond to assumptions about who God is, what is true about the world, the moral status of human beings (including those who are not yet born and those who are dying), and the meaning of human history. How a believer responds to these then determines how he or she makes ethical decisions about death (including issues of euthanasia or when life begins and ends), about what is right or wrong, and how he or she can know anything at all. Sire says,

> The essence of a worldview lies deep in the inner recesses of the human self. A worldview involves the mind, but it is first of all a commitment, a matter of the soul. It is a spiritual orientation more than it is a matter of mind alone (2009, p. 20).

But many Christians do not scrutinize their belief system and instead assume the codes cast upon them. Then when they are called to provide an answer to life's most difficult questions, they can only recite what's been poured into them, and those trials disrupt their foundation. We have been witnesses time after time in crises of people who depart from their religious systems because their beliefs are rooted in shallow ground. We believe that critical reflection forms a fertile soil that nourishes deeply rooted faith.

When believers have tested their suppositions, they hold on bravely and firmly during the stormy passages of life. When our middle son died at less than a week old, we faced a crisis of belief. Many couples that live through the loss of a child are unable to find their way through the grief together, stray from their religious faith, and away from one another, resulting in divorce (Albuquerque, Pereira, & Narciso, 2016). Were it not for our mature faith in Christ, our devout pursuit of God, and our understanding that this served a redemptive purpose, we most likely would have experienced this as well. Everyone will have an existential challenge, and it is then that his or her core resolve and commitment to God are doubted. If people have constructed a solid foundation of beliefs that have faced examination and integration, then the rough waters are easier to navigate.

To incorporate this learning technique, the church community must ensure secure connections between individuals, teachers and participants, and leaders. When this occurs, then learners are motivated to accept the discomfort involved in closely examining their questions and doubts, knowing that they are in a supportive place (Daloz, 2000). In his teaching, Jesus welcomes all of us to come. "But the crowds learned about it and followed him. He welcomed them and spoke to them about the kingdom of God, and healed those who needed healing" (Lk. 9:110). Perhaps healing comes with an honest and vulnerable appraisal of one's heart.

Reflection

It's time to practice some metacognition or how we think about thinking. Consider the following questions.

1. What prevents you or your group from practicing the type of reflection that we suggest? What are the barriers you face?

   _____
   _____
   _____

2. What are the benefits and the disadvantages of critical reflection?

   _____
   _____
   _____

3. How would you suggest implementing this practice into your teaching or class?

   _____
   _____
   _____

CHAPTER 8
HOW DOES THIS WORK?

"Do you see all these great buildings" (Mk. 13:2)?

Some teachers desire practical guidance. We've been theoretical thus far and so want to use this chapter to help you expand your repertoire in implementing the techniques we propose. Remember that discovery teaching is not about imparting information or memorizing facts (Lee, 2006). It's a set of procedures intended to lead to a discovery of how to live a kingdom life. Hopefully, you gained what you needed in Bible study or Sunday school; in other words, the basic stories, important verses, and overall theme of redemption. For those who have not, we suggest you delve into that in a different type of class that covers the Bible. This model of teaching works for those who have the foundation and need to learn how to apply these lessons on a different level. It requires a higher level of thinking. Lee reminds us,

"The success of discovery learning does not depend on the learners' capacity of self-inquiry for completing a task, but on the teachers' teaching methods or strategies for learners to complete a learning task successfully. It is best handled when it is directed and guided by the teacher . . .[who] arranges activities in which the learner searches, manipulates, explores, and investigates" (2006, p. 2).

The discovery method has four phases:

1. Identifying teachable moments;
2. Guiding inquiry with intriguing questions;
3. Allowing exploration of a hypothesis; and
4. Encouraging application (Lee, 2006, p. 3).

In the previous chapters (4, 5, & 6), we explain these, although we add the element of compelling narratives and combine the fourth phase in chapter 7. We determined that these are often inseparable and may happen in combination or sequentially. We want to share the following techniques and activities that contribute to these phases.

Create Teachable Moments

As mentioned previously, several things create teachable moments, including capitalizing on current events, life changes, and unforeseen circumstances. These are difficult to plan, and so we suggest leaders create learner reception. These experiences happen through the power of a narrative, the role of imagination, incorporation of the senses, and engaging the audience's emotions to make the moment memorable. Here are some ways that we do this.

Not everyone is a great storyteller. Some of us are long-winded, and some of us focus on the wrong details. While we wish that all could weave a good yarn, we realize that most of us need a little help with this. In the groups we lead, we depend upon a variety of resources to help us. When we choose a tale, we keep in mind the objective of the lesson. What do we desire that participants walk away with, and how can we enhance their learning experience so that this activity remains with them long enough to bring about change?

We have several books that help us and continually look for others that provide us with the stories we need. One of our favorite books is *Friedman's Fables* by Edwin Friedman (1990). It is a collection of short stories that invite readers to enter conversations about different subjects. One of our favorite tales from this book is "The Bridge" and we have used this in many settings. It offers a choice, and then the discussion can center on the options available and how that might interact with our values, ethics, or spiritual orientation. Another story we use from this book is called "The Power of Belief." It engages participants around the discussion of perceptions. Other books worth mentioning include *The Sower's Seeds: 120 Inspiring Stories for Preaching, Teaching and Public Speaking* (Cavanaugh, 2004), and *Tales of a Magic Monastery* (Theopane, 1981). We've also used children's books, such as *There's No Such Thing as a Dragon* (Kent,

2009), to demonstrate concepts.

Other formats may be better, such as a video, movie, or television clip. We find and save these for group settings. One favorite movie, *Wit,* has a touching part known as "The Popsicle Scene" and portrays a deep conversation for those dealing with a terminal illness (Shore & Campanella, 2007). Another older episode we use is called "Death be not Whatever" from the *Joan of Arcadia* television series (Hall & Hayman, 2003). Other movies and television series have excellent clips that can prompt groups in discourse. We continue to update our video file, although we continue to include some classics due to the success of these within group settings.

The power is in the scene, however, not the whole show or movie. Refrain from the temptation or bequests of your students to watch the entire production. These brief viewings are meant to either prompt or illustrate concepts and to engage the sensory and emotional aspects of the viewer. The follow-up becomes the most memorable moment upon posing questions or hypotheses to the class. We'll discuss this momentarily.

Other teachable moments occur when we offer fun or creative activities. Again, it is not an end to itself but rather a vehicle to guide and enhance the conversation. We have a long list of exercises that we provide, including the use of games, puzzles, mazes, and labyrinths. One activity we use is with a finger labyrinth where we provide copies of a maze and then provide a reading of scripture along with a question as each person comes to a particular spot on their paper. It keeps people engaged, particularly with an extended passage of scripture.

Some other enjoyable exercises we use are children's toys, such as Legos. We do this in several ways. If our goal is to work on group cohesion and yet exemplify diversity, we divide the members into smaller pairs or trios. We provide each group with the same amount and same types of Legos. Then we ask them to construct something. We allow them to share and then lead them in a discussion about their decision-making process and how diversity builds strength. At other times, we'll provide each person with random Legos and let them build something. This discussion may focus then on individuality and the importance of unique talents. This activity is especially good when talking about spiritual gifts.

Other times we will use art as a form of reflection or to describe a spiritual experience or explore theology. Henri Nouwen provides a beautiful meditation on Rembrandt's *The Return of the Prodigal Son* (Nouwen, 1994). We suggest the teacher read this short book and then bring copies of Rembrandt's painting to the class members. Ask them to analyze the picture. What do they see? This exploration may lead to an impressive experience as participants point out all the variations possible while the instructors leads them in a philosophical discussion of the scripture passage or to a personal reflection on which character with whom they most identify. Another painting we love is *The Incredulity of Saint Thomas* by Caravaggio (1602). It's an intriguing portrayal of doubting Thomas that evokes an emotional response and leads to interesting doctrinal discourse. Other pieces of art may spur the same depth of exchange.

At other times, we have used crayons and mandalas for

focus, structured experiences such as human timelines or human barometers, family sculpting to illustrate Biblical genealogies, group murals, or circles of concerns. We've also had individuals bring in personal items, such as favorite hats, a sentimental item, or a recent example of victory over a struggle. Then we invite them to share about these all while interweaving the message into the banter. In all of these, we are attempting to be holistic in our teaching so that everyone walks away, with not only information, but also a tangible involvement in learning. These are the situations that walk out the door and into people's lives as they recall this memory and share it with others.

Asking Good Questions

Some people are adept at asking questions. Others seem to have difficulty with this. The contemplation will only be as meaningful if the inquiry is designed well. Open-ended questions work best for reflection. If you ask a question that someone can respond with a simple yes or no, you've asked a closed question. You want to be sure to ask something that leads to further discussion. Keep in mind that you don't want to use so many questions that participants feel like they're sitting in an exam or are "being grilled." We've found that one or two are enough. Think about the way you initially phrase a question. Here are some examples:

- Tell me why . . . or tell me what might happen if . . .
- Where are you most or least (fill in the blank) . . .

- What are you thinking? What are you feeling?
- In what ways do you believe . . .?
- Explain the following scripture.
- How would it look if we applied this lesson or scripture?
- How would this change your life?
- What barriers prevent you from . . .?

In her article, "Noticing the Duck: The Art of Asking Spiritual Questions," MaryKate Morse mentions four levels of questions: beginnings, ready to go, going deeper, and going deeper still (2009). The first level of items initiate questions that help the believer to recall their relationship with God and may consist of the following:

- Who is the first person who created a memory of God for you?
- What is your earliest experience of God?
- Who is your spiritual hero or role model?
- What is a story from your life that represents the essence of who you are?
- What is a story that represents your current need?
- When you think of God, what picture comes to mind?

As you use these questions, you might think of other ways to phrase these. Some people will be unable to tell a story or feel reticent. Perhaps, you could ask them to share an image of an object or a place that expresses their response. When your class is comfortable at this level of inquiry, you might go to the next level (ready to go) with these questions:

- What is your desire for God?
- What is God's desire for you?
- What are the hindrances?

This query could lead to interesting conversations in the class as people struggle with these. And then you can go to the subsequent level of questions (going deeper):

- What are your predominant feelings about your relationship with God?
- Do you have any internal movements (calls, inclinations, intuitions, initiatives)?
- What blocks are you currently experiencing that are impacting your spiritual walk?
- In what ways are you growing spiritually?
- How do you discern the presence of God in your life?

While Morse suggests the fourth level (going still deeper), we believe those questions should occur on an individual level. They involve using why statements and continuing with those until the person reaches the core of the issue. This line of discourse may not be best suited for class settings due to the vulnerability required and the individual focus that may alienate the answerer from the rest of the group.

A thoughtful study of Jesus' questions will also be helpful. Here are examples of how he worded his questions:

- **If you** . . . ex. If you love those who love you, what reward will you get (Mt. 5:46)?
- **Who** of you . . . or which of you . . . ex. "Who of you by worrying can add a single hour to his life" (Lk. 12:25)?
- **Which** is easier . . . ex. "Which is easier: to say, 'Your sins are forgiven,' or to say, 'Get up and walk'" (Lk. 5:23)?
- **Why** do you . . . ex. "Why do you break the command of God for the sake of your tradition" (Mt. 15:3)?
- **What** . . . ex. "What good will it be for a man [woman] if he [she] gains the whole world, yet forfeits his soul" (Mt. 16:26)?
- **Do** you . . . ex. "Do you still not understand" (Mk. 8:21)?
- **Suppose** . . . ex. "Suppose one of you has a hundred sheep and loses one of them" (Lk. 15:4).
- **Has** . . . or **Haven't** . . . ex. "Has not Moses given you the law" (Jn. 7:19)?

There are some basic types of questions to remember: to test knowledge, comprehension, application, analysis, synthesis, and evaluation (Centre for Teaching Excellence, 2019). Questions about knowledge use who, what, when, where, how, and require brief responses. However, higher-level queries may also use those same words. The difference at this level is the items are merely to ascertain if a person can recall basic facts. To determine comprehension, the teacher needs to ask someone to summarize. When the goal is application, then we move to ask about relationships and making comparisons. "How is Jesus' message about the sheep related to your life?" In the analysis, we want to know if a person is connecting the dots between relationships or concepts. For example, in reading Genesis 3, we might ask in what way are Eve's responses to God related to her interaction with the serpent. In synthesis, the goal is to absorb details and then combine those with concepts; in evaluation we're trying to decipher a person's ability to develop opinions, judgments, or decisions (Centre for Teaching Excellence, 2019).

Another way to understand these levels of questions is understanding types of reflectivity. Mezirow categorizes thinking in the following way:

1. Reflectivity: an awareness of a specific perception, meaning, behavior, or habit.
2. Affective reflectivity: an awareness of how the individual feels about what is being perceived, thought, or acted upon.
3. Discriminant reflectivity: the assessment of the efficacy of perception, thought, action, or habit.
4. Judgmental reflectivity: making and becoming aware of value judgments about perception, thought, action, or habit.
5. Conceptual reflectivity: self-reflecting which might lead to a question of whether good, bad, or adequate concepts were employed for understanding of judgment.
6. Psychic reflectivity: recognition of the habit of making percipient judgments on the basis of limited

information.
7. Theoretical reflectivity: an awareness that the habit for percipient judgment or for conceptual inadequacy lies in a set of taken-for-granted cultural or psychological assumptions which explain personal experience less satisfactorily than another perspective with more functional criteria for seeing, thinking, or acting (1991, p. 12-13).

So as the leader plans the lesson, he or she can decide what type of consideration he or she concludes is best for the class at that time. As you look closely at these seven levels, you will see that they mirror many of Jesus' questions to his disciples, followers, and enemies.

Sometimes we use questions from other sources. One set that we came upon in our work was the Quaker questions, easily adaptable to a variety of situations. They are intended to lead the dialogue deeper. Here are the items: Where did you live between the ages of 5 and 12 and what were the winters like? How was your home heated? What (or who) was the center of warmth in your life when you were a child? When did God become a "warm" being to you and how did this happen? The source for these is unknown and you can find many other versions of these questions. Another resource we use is Gelb's *The How to Think Like Leonardo da Vinci Workbook* (1998). This book contains a treasure of activities that help adults to think in unique ways. One last question we believe encourages deeper reflection is called "The Miracle Question." It's often used in psychotherapy but works very well in any context. While there are many variations, the most common format is the following:

> Suppose when you go to bed tonight and while you are sleeping, a miracle happens and a problem (situation, etc.) is solved. When you awake, what is different? How will you discover the miracle has occurred? What will you notice (Furman)?

One might use a magic wand, or a snap, or something else creative, but this type of question is one that encourages students to develop hypotheses.

Exploring Hypotheses and Application

It is not enough to plan memorable experiences and ask good questions. The goal in discovery teaching is to come full circle at some point so that learners can explore new ideas or hypotheses about faith and then apply that in some way to their lives. If our lessons do not create spiritual re-birth, then we've not accomplished our hearts' desires. The finale is Godly transformation within people. So we provide movements to achieve this.

Some of these actions include creative activities such as making masks, poetry composition, listening to music, producing group murals, reading plays, creating a group prayer, or developing taxonomies of beliefs. Others involve bringing current events or news to the group to actively plan interventions in community settings. We might use role-plays or poetry analysis or case studies to practice application. Or we will sponsor debates to encourage all voices to speak their views on a situation or position.

Of course, while we allow for freedom in exploration, we also prod people to live out the questions, either in their personal lives or corporately in service projects. We don't want to answer all the questions posed. Instead, we desire that people search their hearts, lives, and the world around them for what those questions mean. Sometimes providing straightforward answers to people in the class setting belies them the opportunity of a deeper relationship with God. When the anxiety of ambiguity arises, it has the possibility of driving believers into God's arms. "When we're not open to ambiguity and different ways of looking at things, we risk becoming stagnant, stuck in a cul-de-sac rather than being out on the adventure and open to the mystery of the Divine" (Felten & Procter-Murphy, loc. 186, 2012). In letting people endure the discomfort of unanswered questions, we find ways to bring conversations back to previous lessons as a way to follow-up. It may be necessary to converse with individuals in privacy or to meet outside the class without the limits of time or place.

Reflection

Consider the suggestions in this chapter and respond to the questions below.

1. The discovery model suggests that a teacher identify teachable moments, guide inquiry through good questions, allow exploration, and encourage application. Which of these do you appreciate most? Which are most difficult for you?

   _____
   _____
   _____

2. What activities sound interesting to you? Why?

   _____
   _____
   _____

3. What suggestions help you most in growing spiritually? Why?

   _____
   _____
   _____

PART IV
BEING EXCELLENT

"You are the salt of the earth. But if the salt loses its saltiness, how can it be made salty again" (Mt. 5:13)?

What does it mean to be the type of teacher to whom we refer? Is it possible in the contemporary church to implement the techniques we propose? Our response is, "it depends." To be the person leading this type of group relies upon the openness of a congregation to allow for questions and doubts about doctrine and church practices. Only the most secure churches and leaders can welcome the discourse. Whether this method is possible is conditional to the type of teacher, including personality, ego strength, and motivation. Some are unable to release control, or who are uncomfortable with this style. We respect that there is room in our churches for a variety of groups that fit both teachers and participants.

Some of those who instruct are unable to go this route because of insecurities or unease. That doesn't mean they are not good people or good teachers. Using this discovery approach requires a strong sense of self and one that is unflappable during conflict, controversy, or the increasing discomfort created during the activities. The teacher must practice self-supervision and learn to manage his or her anxiety about the group experience. Then some people are unmotivated to move to this type of teaching. That saddens us, yet we realize that instructors have divergent hopes and wishes for their classes.

We have attempted to impress the importance of changing how we disciple Christian adults. This perspective arises out of our observations, experiences, failed attempts, mistakes, and yet our desire that the churches produce excellent educators, whether they be seminarian graduates or laypeople. The Bible compels us to be exceptional in all that we do. Philippians 4:8 says, "Finally, brothers and sisters, whatever is true, whatever is noble, whatever is right, whatever is pure, whatever is lovely, whatever is admirable – if anything is excellent or praiseworthy – think about such things." It starts with our inner mind and where we choose to focus. But excellence also becomes a matter of heart and habit. Titus 2:7-8 says,

> In everything set them an example by doing what is good. In your teaching show integrity, seriousness and soundness of speech that cannot be condemned, so that those who oppose you may be ashamed because they have nothing bad to say about us.

And Colossians 3:23-24 says,

Whatever you do, work at it with all your heart, as working for the Lord, not for human masters, since you know that you will receive an inheritance from the Lord as a reward. It is the Lord Christ you are serving.

We know that our ministers and churches are increasingly concerned with the lack of knowledge, time, and commitment to the Christian faith. The world in which we live beckons us to respond swiftly to the temptations of life demands. All around us, the non-Christian world holds Christians to a higher standard, and it is our responsibility to exceed those expectations. We must pursue excellence. How does this fit in with our conversation in this book?

If we believe that the church's mission is to go into the entire world and make disciples, then we must find a way to develop a process for spiritual formation that leads to a mission perspective, leading learners to apply the lesson in the world. Sitting in a class, hearing a lecture, or listening to scripture alone is not enough. Beard describes this focus of guiding spiritual formation as, "the experiential process of identity formation which results in a disciple who exhibits tangible evidence of mission, community, and obedience in his or her life" (2015, p. 192). We need people who are willing and know how to effect change in the world, Christians who understand their purpose in their neighborhood, workplace, and city. According to Hirsch (2006), this type of discipleship is not only the acquisition of information and memorization of bible verses; becoming the imitation of Christ does not happen through mimicry, but "through the medium of one's own life" (p. 114).

When we use a discovery model of teaching with adults, the results are impressive because it fosters an enhanced awareness of beliefs, feelings, and critique of perspectives, including the capacity to wisely discern the postmodern messages in the world that have syncretized Christian principles. Being excellent means that the church has a well-formed theory of Christian adult education with clear objectives, learning experiences, effective methods, and avenues for evaluation (Knowles, 1962, p. 74). Becoming excellent in teaching requires a clear understanding of one's approach, goals, modes, and consistent assessment.

For those whose interest is sparked by discovery teaching, we guide you into the compulsory development of these skills. These include the practice of self-reflection, self-supervision, management of physiological reactions, and the use of spiritual practices in preparation for leading. Also, we recommend the recruitment of strong candidates and providing them with training and support. These are the building blocks for a successful adult education program.

CHAPTER 9
WHOSE NEED DOES IT MEET?

*"And if you greet only your own people,
what are you doing more than others" (Mt. 5:47)?*

Self-reflection and self-supervision are critical components in becoming a quality teacher if the goal is to produce spiritually mature adults. Parker Palmer says, "Good teaching cannot be reduced to technique; good teaching comes from the identity and integrity of the teacher" (1998, p. 10). It is in the practice of examining one's self, motivations, and desires that growth occurs.

To lead adults successfully, one must ponder the following: what do I believe? Can I teach something I do not believe? What is my personality? What aspects of my personality contribute to my teaching in a positive way, and what character defaults get in the way of my teaching? What spiritual practices do I believe enhance my instruction and how well do I observe those? Why do I want to lead groups? When I do teach, whose need am I meeting? Is it my need or the needs of the participants? All these questions call for you to be straightforward with yourself.

Most of us function with a dichotomous view of ourselves. We see the ideal, the best qualities we embrace and desire for others to see, and yet we recognize our weaknesses and hope that others do not notice those. If we're truthful with ourselves, we appreciate those things about us that are changeable, are likely to change, and those that we are not interested in growing, and those that are unlikely to develop. Whether you use personality inventories or feedback from your family, friends, or peers, or hopefully both, the information provides you the chance to think about who you are and what you desire.

Frequently in supervision with our ministry and counseling students, we use case study reviews to demonstrate their skills and reveal their motivations. It is typical for us to ask why a student does a particular thing. "Why did you pray for Jim? Was it helpful to him or not? Did it make you feel good?" The underlying incentive is thereby determined. If you desire to teach because you like it and it makes you feel good about yourself, then we remain supportive of you. We're not saying that's an inadequate reason. What we do want you to know is that self-motivation will then impact your objectives, procedures, and potentially your students' growth. We genuinely want you to be clear about why you are doing this. The follow-up question pertains to your sense of calling. Are you called to teach? Who called you? Or are you teaching because the church needs someone, and you are filling the spot? If this is true, we ask that you prayerfully consider if that is the appropriate place of service.

Teachers must disregard their personal need to complete a curriculum, and instead, concentrate on the genuine spiritual development of their students. Adults need time – time to think, to question, to integrate what they read and hear. This process is what produces long-lasting transformation. The question for the teacher becomes: for what purpose do I teach? If the aim is to shepherd God's people, then the goal for the group or class alters.

Sometimes in our enthusiasm or desire to please others, we accept the task of leading a class only to find that we dread preparation and attendance. That's not the place to be because that impedes the learning progress of participants. Members of the group sense when a teacher is unprepared, unwilling, or unmotivated. It communicates a lack of support and quickly quenches the thirst for biblical education and application. If you don't want to teach, learn to say no. There are plenty of other areas where you can serve, and setting these boundaries maintains your authenticity.

When you teach, it is incumbent upon you to strengthen your level of spirituality and increase your dependence upon God. Otherwise, you will soon grow weary, and teaching will become burdensome. The successful teacher must be aware of these creeping feelings and act instantly to re-engage in their efforts. When this happens, most people assume the best option is to "take a break;" however, reconnection is the antidote. In studies of burnout, the most prominent factor in prevention and overcoming this type of stress is engagement (Maslach, 2016).

The third consideration is how you will define success in

your teaching. What is most important to you? Do you desire that your class increase in numbers? Or do you hope that members will become actively engaged in programs that reach out to marginalized people? Do you want the group to be a place for fun and engagement and fellowship? Perhaps, you envision that people will become healthy and strong Christians. Again, we are not trying to tell you what your aim should be, but rather that your ambitions be clear and obtainable. What will you do if that's not possible, or it doesn't happen? How are you going to evaluate your teaching and the accomplishments of the group?

Another factor to consider is that of ego strength. This is a psychological term used to describe one's ability for judgment, reality testing, successful relationships, response to feedback and criticism, and the capacity for change (Bjorklund, 2000). It's important in teaching because it allows one to perform critical reflection. Brookfield says,

> To some extent, we are all prisoners trapped within the perceptual frameworks that determine how we view our experiences. A self-confirming cycle often develops whereby our uncritically accepted assumptions shape actions that then only serve to confirm the truth of those assumptions. We find it very difficult to stand outside ourselves and see how some of our most deeply held values and beliefs lead us into distorted and constrained ways of being (1998, p. 197).

When a person has lower self-esteem, then he or she will lack the confidence, ability to connect successfully in relationships and will be swept away by emotional turmoil or lack of progress (Peterson, 2015). The intensity of group dynamics will overwhelm this teacher.

Supervision of one's self, including personality, motivation, and ambitions is a requirement. If you do not work on these, then you will find yourself forcing a group to practice critical reflection when they are resistant.

> Adult learners will react quite negatively to a teacher's attempts to make them more critically reflective. In such cases, teachers should respect the learner's individuality and remember that adult education is a collaborative, transactional encounter . . . Teachers who are proselytizing ideologues are really not teachers at all; they measure their success solely by the extent to which learners come to think like them, not by the learner's development of a genuine questioning and critical outlook" (Brookfield, 1986, p. 126).

When leaders embrace their self-reflection, then they become clear about their calling and purpose and their availability to attend to and discern group development needs.

Reflection

It's time to review and evaluate your investment in teaching.

1. Why do you teach? Is it a desire or calling?

   _____
   _____
   _____

2. What do you hope will be the result or accomplishments of your teaching?

   _____
   _____
   _____

3. How can you determine when, where, and what type of class or group to lead?

   _____
   _____
   _____

CHAPTER 10
INNER & OUTER ATTENDING

"How can you say to your brother, 'Let me take the speck out of your eye,' when all the time there is a plank in your own eye" (Mt. 7:4)?

Sometimes a class may become tense. If the teacher is practicing the discovery method, this will happen frequently. This occurrence can be uncomfortable for the one leading the class and can increase the group anxiety if not managed well. Exploring the depths of belief systems can be precarious. Participants will look to the leader for cues of whether or not the group can handle the disequilibrium. There are several practices that a teacher can adopt to achieve a balance of tension and relief. The objective is to maintain enough destabilization to move people to discovery of new concepts but not so much that people shut down cognitively or emotionally. This balance requires skill in both inner and outer attending.

Those who teach in educational settings are quite familiar with classroom management. Here we are referring to how the leader can facilitate healthy discussions while paying attention to their physiological arousal as well as noticing how the class is reacting. Whenever we provide adults the freedom to choose how they learn and encourage critical reflection, we must be prepared when those participants challenge our constructs that are part of our identity. For example, if you are talking about a controversial topic, such as abortion, and you have a strong belief that supports pro-life measures, and a church member disagrees, or perhaps simply explores that alternative position, you will most likely feel the tension and the need to "correct" this person's statement. At the very least, you may feel defensive even if you don't respond. This type of tension will happen often, and the teacher must learn to manage his or her reaction.

Whenever someone poses an argument that is opposite our own, naturally we feel a sense of threat. That will trigger a physiological response that increases our blood pressure, heart rate, and cortisol that makes us feel physically uncomfortable. The first step is simply noticing what one experiences in his or her body in response to participant statements and questions. The next step is reminding oneself that there is no actual risk. Our bodies were created to respond to real or perceived hazards. If a hungry tiger walks in the room, we definitely will be looking to run, fight, or hide. However, if we only imagine the tiger is there, then we can convince ourselves that there is no danger, and we can use some self-soothing techniques to overcome our fear. The final step is a re-orientation of our physical state. The body returns to resting state when we breathe deeply, change our posture, or move to a different place in the room. We also suggest that listening without evaluating whether the comment is good or bad, right or wrong, biblical or not, will move us more quickly to physical recovery.

It is important to remain calm – that is what the crowd will notice. How do we react during these times? When a participant says or does something that activates our sympathetic nervous system, we can learn to control the reactivity of our bodies, mind, and emotions. Practicing this calming technique inside and outside class will relieve the tension. We have witnessed how teachers will quickly abandon an intense discussion due to their anxiety.

Part of what also needs to occur is the use of calming words and activities for the class as well. This moment is where well-placed humor or inviting others into the conversation may be helpful. Or it may be beneficial to introduce an artifact or activity, but not to deter from the discussion but rather to enhance it. Going back to the example of our abortion discussion, perhaps you could mention a recent news article, book, or movie. It's important to communicate to the dissident that his or her thoughts are welcome and we want to explore those further. This way, we are honoring the differing stance but relieving a bit of the stress. Doing this is an art, and the best way to learn is through observation of leaders who do this well. The key is allowing the discussion to continue. Do not redirect, or subvert the discourse or the underlying message to the group will be that dissimilarity of opinion is unacceptable. Let conflict arise, ease some of the tension, and then aid the class in discovering how they can support one another. Notice we don't say they need to agree. That's unnecessary, but we do want the members to appreciate and respect one another.

During times of intense discussion, be aware that others will experience physiological arousal as well. If this happens too much or becomes too intense, they will choose to forego the class because it takes an emotional toll on all present. However, the leader who notices when this occurs and provides an outlet for excessive stress will then reassure and comfort people that all is under control. There are times when the teacher needs to check in with class members after a heated discussion.

The alert leader is watching all members in the room, observing to see if anyone appears flooded or overwhelmed. Watch for physical clues such as shallow breathing, tense muscles, hyperactivity such as jiggling a foot or moving around in one's seat, and defensive postures such as crossing one's arms or turning away from the group. If these are changes that occur during the discussion, they may signal that the individual is having some physical discomfort. Unease may appear in their tone of voice if it becomes tight, higher or lower, more rapid, slower, or if their enunciation becomes more pronounced. These are warning signs that they need a bit of reprieve, and the instructor can help through modeling tranquility and performing metacommunication. It may be as simple as, "It seems that this is a touchy subject. Who would like to talk about their thoughts or feelings?" We don't want to ease the pressure too much or too quickly or the power of the moment may be lost. We do want to acknowledge how this conversation is awkward and encourage people to wade through the muddy dialogue with us. Reminding them they are not alone and that we will accompany them, lending a hand where needed, will often provide enough reassurance.

Another tool readily available to any teacher is the use of silence. It can be used to provoke or calm a group. It takes only a few seconds of quietness to get a class talking but can be risky unless people have received some directive or a stated question. When someone attempts to inquiry in a direction that is opposite of where the leader desires to move, then a moment of silence offers the questioner the chance to redirect their thought. Or when the tension becomes great, reticence demonstrates a sense of composed thoughtfulness. Silence is a form of communication. It can be threatening or feel awkward at times.

Palmer says, "We need to abandon the notion that 'nothing is happening' when it is silent, to see how much new clarity a silence often brings" (1993, p. 80). There are moments of quiet that bring new energy or vision. It can be a way of establishing order or redistributing power in a group (Trahan, 2013). Annobil and Thompson say,

> Meticulous use of silence is a powerful tool because it encourages listening, removes barriers between teacher and learner and creates space for multiple ways of knowing instead of word-based knowledge acquisition. Teachers who fear repressive silence may equate noise with active learning. However, sometimes educators need to step back from activity and reconsider the possibility of silence (2017, p. 325).

The sage instructor understands the influence present in the absence of words and chooses those moments to wield intentional direction. With the use of emotion management and silence, the leader becomes a non-anxious presence or container in the room that holds the overflow of apprehension in such a way that members feel safe to pour out their most complex uncertainties.

Reflection

Let's think further about attention to your physiological responses and group reactions.

1. How does your body tell you when something is a stressful topic? What does your anxiety tell you about yourself and/or the group? What's your immediate reaction?

   _____
   _____
   _____

2. In what ways have leaders demonstrated to you that conflict can be managed well in group settings?

   _____
   _____
   _____

3. How have you experienced silence? How can you be more comfortable with it?

   _____
   _____
   _____

CHAPTER 11
TRAINING & SUPPORTING REFLECTIVE TEACHERS

"You of little faith, why are you so afraid" (Mt. 8:26)?

In our research and experience, we notice that there is a scarcity of information in training church instructors in the model and methods we suggest. We know how to perform in this manner due to our reading, and through the supervision we receive and offer to students. There is literature on adult pedagogy, but most of it pertains to higher education. We cannot assume that lay leaders will have the same level of interest, or time, to investigate this mode. Yet some may wonder how and where they begin. A person's qualities and personality are part of the success. Parker Palmer's advice for teacher development includes building trust, investing time, providing opportunities for exploration in teaching, feedback regarding style, and brainstorming (1992). We have several thoughts about the recruitment, training, and on-going support for those who desire to teach adults.

Ideal Recruits

It is a difficult task for church leadership to find willing volunteers. We do not envy their position and realize it requires an on-going pursuit. In our experiences as church ministry staff, we were happy to have almost anyone who offered their support. There were times when we needed to fill a spot, and few were willing or able to make that commitment. However, we also don't want to mistake inclination with competence. Not all people will enjoy teaching, and some are not yet ready for that task. There are some common characteristics that help us define a solid choice for the position. One imperative trait is intellectual capacity, along with thinking flexibility. A person who desires to lead adults needs a sharp focus and the adaptability necessary to re-route the group in the middle of the process. Those people who struggle with higher-order thinking or those who desire to control the process too tightly will become easily frustrated or will exasperate the group. One needs to be a step ahead of the mental progression and change directions instantly if required. The teacher may need to abandon the preplanned lesson in favor of the unfolding process of discovery.

Another vital attribute is openness to growth and challenge. As previously mentioned, self-reflection and self-supervision provide a conducive environment for learning. If we think about the phases necessary for growth, then we need leaders who are mindful of the subtleties of these stages and can identify the needs of individuals. Lee states, "The process of learning is not simply accepting the teachers' idea or explanation. It is active knowledge construction" (2010, p. 72). This dynamic process of testing hypotheses involves moving through transitions that require the leader's constant evaluation throughout the transformation. As people grow, the teacher must guide them through inspiration and facilitation of the education experience, while allowing participants to discover new possibilities. Then the facilitator must encourage occasions for the adult to apply the fresh views and change the world around them (Lee, 2010).

In searching for competent and confident teachers, church leaders need to know their congregational members. One does not need magnificent oration or presentation skills. Teaching in this way is a matter of the heart. Those who are best suited for this type of education are people who invite differing outlooks, know how to connect knowledge and information with experience, can discern predominant themes, and are devoted to foster lifelong learning in their class members (Brown, 2009).

Training

How does one train others in this method? We believe the best training occurs through modeling and supervision. While we offer a variety of resources for leaders to examine and encourage reading, this alone is insufficient. Earlier, we suggest ideas for activities, and these are helpful but operate only as the means to an end. The training of excellent teachers begins by imparting a theory about how spiritual formation occurs in adults and continuing with guiding the skill development in reflective practice. Zanzig (2012) has a model of spiritual development that he calls the Spirituality Wheel. He views spiritual growth as cyclical moving from spiritual hunger to search, then awakening, and finally, response. As adults encounter different dimensions of life and move through developmental stages, the evolution repeats until all experiences and concepts are integrated (Zanzig, 2012). Training should include an overview of the various theories of adult learning and representative models. This task occurs in an introductory course in leading adult groups.

The more significant duty is to provide mentors to help teachers formulate a solid theory, develop insightful inquiry skills, provide guidance, and demonstrate ways to handle difficult situations. We believe that pairing a new facilitator with a practiced one best accomplishes the mission. They can learn from one another as they share ideas. The skillful leader can show how learning moves through phases of engagement, exploration, explanation, elaboration, and evaluation (Robertson, 2008). In doing so, conversations that consider the type of curriculum, experiential practices, and questions occur. Clarification can be the result, and experimentation can proceed.

Support

The best educational programs provide on-going support for their teachers. Providing novel learning experiences through additional resources can bring fresh material. Praying for and checking with leaders is crucial. It is essential to communicate that facilitators are not alone; they are part of a broader community invested in their success, as well as the growth of individual class members. Being on the alert for signs for burnout will prevent groups from deteriorating. This awareness is both a teacher and leadership responsibility. Providing retreats, respite, or re-education may be necessary. We previously mentioned the primacy of engagement. Reconnection requires the facilitator to continue to examine and listen for God's voice in a reaffirmation of the calling to teach. Reengagement also entails connecting more deeply rather than pulling back, as the tendency occurs. Listening attentively and using one's empathy reinvigorates the leader (Miller & Sprang, 2016).

Finding the right leaders is an investment of the church in the spiritual formation of its members. When adults receive appropriate and engaging education and support in their spiritual growth, they become the light in the world to which Jesus calls us. The final testament of quality church tutelage becomes apparent as believers move from their Sunday chair and enter the platform of the world at large, bringing the Gospel message of Christ, and sharing evolutionary principles that bring systemic change. Jesus sums this up in his prayer for believers in John 17:20-26:

> "My prayer is not for them alone. I pray also for those who will believe in me through their message, that all of them may be one, Father, just as you are in me and I am in

you. May they also be in us so that the world may believe that you have sent me. I have given them the glory that you gave me, that they may be one as we are one — I in them and you in me — so that they may be brought to complete unity. Then the world will know that you sent me and have loved them even as you have loved me. Father, I want those you have given me to be with me where I am, and to see my glory, the glory you have given me because you loved me before the creation of the world. Righteous Father, though the world does not know you, I know you, and they know that you have sent me. I have made you known to them, and will continue to make you known in order that the love you have for me may be in them and that I myself may be in them."

Reflection

We have come to the end of our proposal and invite your collaboration in this last reflection.

1. What obstacles prevent your church from adopting this method?

   _____
   _____
   _____

2. How could you approach this topic with your church leaders? What would convince them of this modification to your adult program?

   _____
   _____
   _____

3. What lingering questions or thoughts do you have upon completion of this book? Are there suggestions you desire or intend to implement?

   _____
   _____
   _____

Bibliography

Albuquerque, S., Pereira, M., & Narciso, J. (2016). Couple's relationship after the death of a child: A systematic review. *Journal of Child & Family Studies, 25*(1), 30.

Allen, R. N., & Jackson, A. R. (2017). Contemporary teaching strategies: Effectively engaging millennials across the curriculum [pdf file]. *University of Detroit Mercy Law Review, 95*(1), 1-33.

Annobil, C. N., & Thompson, M. (2017). Educational theories inherent in Jesus Christ's pedagogical techniques and their implications for implementing the early childhood curriculum [pdf file]. *International Conference on Education, Development & Innovation, 2017*, Seville, Spain.

Armstrong, P. (2016). Bloom's taxonomy.

Barrett, T. (2015, Feb 11). Learning provocations (ideas, how they affect us and why we should use them)[blog].

Beard, C. B. (2015). Missional discipleship: Discerning spiritual-formation practices and goals within the missional movement. *Missiology, 43*(2), 175-194.

Bjorklund, P. (2000). Assessing ego strength: Spinning straw into gold. *Perspectives in Psychiatric Care, 36*(1), 14-23.

Bloom, B. S. (ed.). (1956). *Taxonomy of educational objectives: Book 1 cognitive domain*. Saddle River, NJ: Addison Wesley Longman, Inc.

Bonhoeffer, D. (1959). *The cost of discipleship* (trans. München). Norwich, UK: SCM Press Ltd.

Bosanquet, S. (Producer), & Nichols, M. (Director). (2001). *Wit* [motion picture]. United States: HBO Films.

Boucher, M. I. (1981). *The parables.* Wilmington, DE: Michael Glazier Publisher.

Breen, M. (2015). *Choosing to learn from life.* Greenville, SC: 3DM International.

Bristol, T., & Isaac, E. P. (2009). Christian education and constructivism: Learning through the adult Sunday school class. Presentation at the *Adult Education Research Conference*: Chicago, IL.

Brookfield, S. D. (1986). *Understanding and facilitating adult learning.* San Francisco, CA: Jossey Bass.

Brookfield, S. D. (1995). *Becoming a critically reflective teacher.* San Francisco, CA: Jossey Bass.

Brookfield, S. (1998, Fall). Critically reflective practice. *Journal of Continuing Education in the Health Professions, 18*(4), 197-205.

Brown, K. (2009). Questions for the 21st century learner. *Knowledge Quest, 38*(1), 24-27.

Bryant, D. (2017). Luke's disruptive Jesus: Harnessing the power of disruptive leadership [pdf file]. *Journal of Biblical Perspectives in Leadership, 7*(1), 145-162.

Bryson, J. D. (2013). Engaging adult learners: Philosophy, principles and practices [pdf file].

Byrd, N. (2011, Nov 1). Narrative discipleship: Guiding emerging adults to "Connect the Dots" of life and faith. *Christian Education Journal: Research on Educational Ministry, 8*(2), 244-262.

Caravaggio, M. (1602). The incredulity of saint Thomas [painting]. Sanssouci, Potsdam, Germany.

Cavanaugh, B. (2004). *The sower's seed: 120 inspiring stories for preaching, teaching and public speaking.* Mahway, NJ: Paulist Press.

Centre for Teaching Excellence, University of Waterloo. (2019). Asking questions: Six types.

Chaves, E. de C. L., de Carvalho, E. C., Beijo, L. A., Goyatá, S. L. T., & Pillon, S.C. (2011). Efficacy of different instruments for the identification of the nursing diagnosis spiritual distress. *Revista Latino-Americana de Enfermagem (RLAE), 19*(4), 902 – 910.

Chong, L. C. (2018, Aug 16). Making sense of Jesus' countercultural teachings.

Chowdhury, M. S. (2006, Jun). Human behavior in the context of training: An overview of the role of learning applied to training and development. *Journal of Knowledge Management Practice, 7*(2).

Daloz, L. A. (2000). Transformative learning for the common good. In Mezirow, *Learning as transformation* (pp. 71-102). San Francisco, CA: Jossey Bass.

Easterday, M. (2016, Dec 22). OPINION: Teachable moments: For America's colleges, the future of coaching is now.

Espinor, D. (2010). Overview of learning theories (ch. 1). In H. Lee, *Faith-based education that constructs: A creative dialogue between constructivism and faith-based education* pp. 5-21). Eugene, OR: Wipf & Stock.

Espinoza, B. D. (2013). The Christian story and our stories: Narrative pedagogy in congregational life. *Christian Education Journal, 10*(2), 432- 443.

Estes, D. C. (2013). *The questions of Jesus in John: Logic, rhetoric, and persuasive discourse.* Leiden, Neth.: Koninklijke Brill NV.

Felten, D., & Proctor-Murphy, J. (2012). *Living the questions: The wisdom or progressive Christianity.* San Francisco, CA: HarperOne Publisher.

Foote, L. S. (2015). Re-storying life as a means of critical reflection: The power of narrative learning. *Christian Higher Education, 14*(3), 116-126.

Friedman, E. H. (1990). *Friedman's fables.* New York, NY: The Guilford Press.

Furman, B. (n.d.). Varieties of the miracle question.

Gagliardi, G. (n.d.). Jesus's humor [online blog].

Gelb, M. J. (1998). *The how to think like Leonardo da Vinci workbook.* New York, NY: Dell Publishing.

Hall, B. (Writer), & Levin, P. (Director). (2003, Nov 7). Death be not whatever [television series]. In B. Hall & J. Hayman (Executive Producers), *Joan of Arcadia.* Los Angeles, CA: CBS Television Distribution.

Hampton, J. K. (2016). Using narrative to invite others into the story of God. In T. Linhart (ed.), *Teaching the next generations: A comprehensive guide for teaching Christian formation.* Grand Rapids, MI: Baker Academic.

Heliand, R., & Hjalmarson, L. (2011). *Missional spirituality: Embodying God's love from the inside out.* Downers Grove, IL: InterVarsity Press.

Hirsch, A., & Hirsch, D. (2010). *Untamed: Reactivating a missional form of discipleship.* Grand Rapids, MI: Baker Books.

Jagerson, J. (2014). Harnessing the power of narrative: Literacy and orality in Christian education. *Christian Education Journal, 11*(2), 259 – 275.

Jones, L. B. (1995). *Jesus, CEO.* New York, NY: Hyperion.

Klimes, H. (n.d.). Spiritual care: Help in distress [online course].

Knowles, M. S. (1962). A theory of Christian adult education methodology. In L. C. Little (Ed.), *Wider horizons in Christian adult education* (pp. 73-87). Pittsburgh, PA: University of Pittsburgh Press.

Knowles, M. S., Holton, E. F., Swanson, R. A. (1998). *The adult learner: The definitive classic in adult education and human resource development* (5th ed.). Woburn, MA: Butterworth-Heineman.

Lavender, E. (2014). My story, our story, God's story: The function of a livable narrative in spiritual formation. *Leaven, 22*(1), 1-4.

Lawrence, R. L., & Paige, D. S. (2016). What our ancestors knew: Teaching and learning through storytelling. In C. R. Nanton (Ed.), *Tectonic boundaries: Negotiating convergent forces in adult education, 149.* Danvers, MA: Wiley Periodicals.

Lee, H. (2006). Jesus teaching through discovery. *International Christian Community of Teacher Educators Journal, 1*(2), 1-7.

Lee, H. & Givens, R. (2012). Critical consciousness and the Christian consciousness: Making the necessary connection between faith-based learning and critical pedagogy. *Journal of research of Christian Education, 21*(3). 195-210.

Lee, H., & Roso, C. G. (2010). Jesus and Bloom: How effective was Jesus in requiring people to think critically? In H. Lee, *Faith-based education that constructs: A creative dialogue between constructivism and faith-based education.* Eugene, OR: Wipf & Stock.

MacCormack, P. (2013, Oct 31). Thin moments [blog].

Manternach, D. P. (2002, Jul). Fostering reflective teachers in a globalized age. *Religious Education, 97*(3), 271-287.

Maslach, C. (2016). Understanding the burnout experience: Recent research and its implications for psychiatry. *World Psychiatry, 15*(2), 103-111.

McCoy, J. W. (2016). The teaching methods of Jesus. *The Journal of Biblical Foundations of Faith and learning, 1*(1), art. 9.

McIntosh, E. (2018). 'Provoke me if you want me to learn' [online blog].

McKenzie, L., & Harton, R. M. (2002). *The religious education of adults.* Macon, GA: Smyth & Helwys Books.

Mezirow, J. (1997, Sum). Transformative learning: Theory to practice [pdf file]. *New Directions for Adult and Continuing Education, 74,* 5-12.

Miller, B., & Sprang, G. (2016, Jan). A components-based practice and supervision model for reducing compassion fatigue by affecting clinician experience. *Traumatology, 23*(2), 153-164.

Morse, M. (2009). Noticing the duck: The art of asking spiritual questions. *Faculty publications – George Fox Evangelical Seminary,* no. 22.

Nicoll, W. R. (1897). *The expositor's Greek testament.* New York, NY: George H. Duran Publishing.

Nouwen, H. (1994). *The return of the prodigal son: A story of homecoming.* New York, NY: Doubleday.

O'Sullivan, E., Morrell, A., & O'Connor, M. (Eds.). (2004).

Expanding the boundaries of transformative learning. New York, NY: Palgrave Macmillan.

Ozuah, P. O. (2005). First, there was pedagogy and then came andragogy. *Einstein Journal of Biology & Medicine, 21*(2), 83-87.

Pappas, C. (2013). The adult learning theory – andragogy – of Malcolm Knowles.

Palmer, P. J. (1992). Reflections on a program for "The Formation of Teachers" [pdf file]. Kalamazoo, MI: Fetzer Institute.

Palmer, P. (1993). *To know as we are known: Education as a spiritual journey* (2nd ed.). New York, NY: HarperCollins.

Palmer, P. (1998). *The courage to teach: Exploring the inner landscape of a teacher's life.* San Francisco, CA: John Wiley & Sons.

Peterson, S. (2015, Dec 16). The mindful ego. *Grand Canyon University.*

Piaget, J. (1985). *The equilibrium of cognitive structures: The central problem of intellectual development.* Chicago: University of Chicago Press.

Platt, D. (2010). *Radical: Taking back your faith from the American dream.*
Colorado Springs, CO: Multonomah Books.

Roberto, J., & Minkiewicz, C. (2007). Best practices in adult faith formation [pdf file], p. 9.

Rule, P. N. (2017). The pedagogy of Jesus in the parable of the Good Samaritan: A diacognitive analysis. *HTS Teologiese Studies,* (3).

Sanders, D. (2018). From critical thinking to spiritual maturity: Connecting the apostle Paul and John Dewey. *Christian Education Journal, 15*(1), 90-104.

Shore, D. (Writer), & Campanella, J. J. (Director). (2007, Jan 30). One day, one room [television series]. In D. Shore (Executive Producer), *House*. Los Angeles, CA: 20th Century Fox Studios.

Sire, J. (2009). *The universe next door: A basic worldview catalog* (5th ed.). Downers Grove, IL: InterVarsity Press.

Snodgrass, K. (2008). *Stories with intent: A comprehensive guide to the parables of Jesus*. Grand Rapids, MI: Wm. B. Eerdmans Publishing Co.

Theopane. (1981). *Tales of a magic monastery*. Chestnut Ridge, NJ: Crossroads Publishing.

Trahan, H. A. (2013, Jun). The silent teacher: A performative, meditative model of pedagogy. *Liminalties: A Journal of Performance Studies, 9*(3). van Rijn, R. (1661-1669). The return of the prodigal son [painting]. Hermitage Museum, Saint Petersburg, Russia.

Warden, M.D. (1998). Extraordinary results from ordinary teachers: learning to teach as Jesus taught. Loveland, CO: Group.

Weiner, E. (2012, Mar 9). Where heaven and earth come closer. *The New York Times*.

Wu, J. (2015). How would Jesus tell it? Crafting stories from an honor-shame perspective [pdf file]. *Evangelical Missions Quarterly*.

Yancey, P. (1988). *Disappointment with God: Three questions no one asks aloud*. Grand Rapids, MI: Zondervan.

Zanzig, T. (2012, Fall). Spiritual transformation: The heart of adult faith formation [pdf file].

About the Authors

Kathy Hoppe is a licensed marital and family therapist, adjunct faculty member, minister, and conference leader. She has worked in the fields of mental health and ministry in private, group, hospital, medical centers, hospices, and employee assistance programs. She has taught undergraduate and graduate courses at seven universities. She has a Doctor of Ministry from Oral Roberts University, a Master of Divinity from Golden Gate Baptist Theological Seminary, a Master of Science in general psychology from Grand Canyon University, and a Bachelor of Arts in psychology from the University of North Texas. Additionally, she is a certified compassion fatigue specialist and has a certificate in online teaching and learning and a postgraduate certificate in marriage and family therapy approved by the Commission on Marriage and Family Therapy Education (COAMFTE).

Jeff Hoppe is a chaplain and ACPE Certified Educator. His experience spans 40 years as a church starter, pastor, senior pastoral care director, and ACPE Supervisor/Certified Educator in hospital settings across the United States. ACPE is the premier Department of Education recognized organization that provides high quality clinical pastoral education programs and training for spiritual care professionals of all faiths through a rigorous accreditation process. Also, Jeff has also served as adjunct faculty at several seminaries. In addition to his certification, Jeff has a Master of Divinity from Golden Gate Baptist Theological

Seminary and a Bachelor of Arts in communication from Baylor University.

Together their service in ministry, training pastoral leaders, and education of adult learners totals almost 80 years. They were initially attracted because of their deep conversations and lack of fear of exploring uncomfortable topics. They continue to have interesting discussions and remain faithful best friends.

Made in the USA
Columbia, SC
23 November 2019